Security Careers

Third Edition

T0348735

Security Careers

Skills, Compensation, and Career Paths

Third Edition

Stephen W. Walker

James E. Foushée

ELSEVIER

AMSTERDAM • BOSTON • HEIDELBERG • LONDON
NEW YORK • OXFORD • PARIS • SAN DIEGO
SAN FRANCISCO • SINGAPORE • SYDNEY • TOKYO

Security
Executive Council

Elsevier
225 Wyman Street, Waltham, MA, 02451, USA
The Boulevard, Langford Lane, Kidlington, Oxford, OX5 1GB, UK

Originally published by the Security Executive Council
First edition, 2006
Second edition, 2009
Copyright © 2014 The Security Executive Council. Published by Elsevier Inc. All rights reserved.

Notices
Knowledge and best practice in this field are constantly changing. As new research and experience broaden our understanding, changes in research methods or professional practices, or medical treatment may become necessary.

Practitioners and researchers must always rely on their own experience and knowledge in evaluating and using any information or methods, compounds, or experiments described herein. In using such information or methods they should be mindful of their own safety and the safety of others, including parties for whom they have a professional responsibility.

To the fullest extent of the law, neither the Publisher nor the authors, contributors, or editors, assume any liability for any injury and/or damage to persons or property as a matter of products liability, negligence or otherwise, or from any use or operation of any methods, products, instructions, or ideas contained in the material herein.

Library of Congress Cataloging-in-Publication Data
Walker, Stephen W.
    Security careers : skills, compensation, and career paths / Stephen W. Walker, James E. Foushée. – Third edition.
        pages cm
        ISBN 978-0-12-800104-2
1. Security consultants. 2. Business enterprises–Security measures. 3. Computer networks–Security measures. 4. Fraud--Prevention. I. Foushée, James E. II. Title.
    HD61.5.W35 2014
    005.8023--dc23
                                          2013045270

British Library Cataloguing-in-Publication Data
A catalogue record for this book is available from the British Library

ISBN: 978-0-12-800104-2

For more publications in the Elsevier Risk Management and Security Collection, visit our website at store.elsevier.com/SecurityExecutiveCouncil.

This book has been manufactured using Print On Demand technology. Each copy is produced to order and is limited to black ink. The online version of this book will show color figures where appropriate.

Printed and bound by CPI Group (UK) Ltd, Croydon, CR0 4YY

Working together to grow libraries in developing countries

www.elsevier.com • www.bookaid.org

Contents

Acknowledgments

The concept for this book was developed by Bob Hayes, managing director of the Security Executive Council.

About the Authors

Stephen W. Walker

Mr. Walker is the senior partner of the Foushée Group, Inc. He has more than 18 years of experience in the management-consulting field. He specializes in incentive plan design and implementation, salary and wage administration program development, and compensation survey design and development.

In the field of compensation, Mr. Walker has managed projects in a variety of industries including high technology, engineering services, information systems, national laboratories, pharmaceutical, energy, and venture capital. He has worked with senior management to review and develop compensation programs that are designed to serve the business objectives and management philosophies unique to each organization.

Mr. Walker holds a BS in business administration, and is a former Commissioned Officer in the United States Marine Corps. He is a frequent lecturer to professional and business groups, author, faculty member for the Security Executive Council, and is a member of a variety of human resources and compensation organizations. In 2009, Mr. Walker was voted one of the most influential people in security by *Security* magazine.

James E. Foushée

Mr. Foushée has over 30 years of experience in the management consulting profession. Currently, he is the managing director of the Foushée Group, Inc., which he founded in 1980 to provide consulting services in all aspects of compensation program design and in organization analysis, planning, and structuring. The firm serves a wide variety of high technology manufacturing, transportation, retail/wholesale, and financial services companies. Client companies range from start-up and emerging firms to Fortune 500 corporations.

For the past 30 years, the firm's staff has focused its efforts in the research of pay practices of environmental, health, safety, security, ethics, and business conduct occupations. Their experience in this endeavor has provided them with a unique expertise to produce America's only comprehensive studies of compensation practices in the environmental, health and safety, and security and compliance fields.

Mr. Foushée holds graduate degrees in business management and psychology. He is a frequent lecturer to professional and business groups and is active in a variety of professional and civic organizations.

Introduction

Lack of research and documentation of sustainable practices has plagued the security industry for years. There is no documentation of the state of the security industry. There are pieces, but it is splintered by various subgroups' views—the practitioner, security equipment manufacturer, consultant/integrator, the corporation that employs security professionals and government agencies that work with all of the former to protect the nation from risk.

Security Careers: Skills, Compensation, and Career Paths provides the comprehensive overview of security industry careers that has previously been lacking. *Security Careers* was originally developed as a part of the Security Executive Council State of the Industry series, which includes current research for understanding and communicating the critical elements of a security issue and how the industry is responding to it.

Security Careers is the only source of security career job descriptions and pay practices of security, compliance, and ethics occupations. The job descriptions and compensation ranges in this report are drawn from research from the Foushée Group, which has been conducting this research since 1980.

The purpose of this book is to help you with your career and your security program. Use the information contained herein to help you to clearly define your roles and responsibilities, your worth, and your career path, thereby enabling you to clearly and precisely delineate your employment position. If you are a manager, use it for staff planning to fill existing or new positions and to validate pay structures.

The job descriptions and compensation trending graphs included in this book are based on many years of research specific to the security function; use this unbiased information with your corporate colleagues that may be unfamiliar with the scope and scale of particular security positions. While this book is more intended for existing security professionals who want to get ahead, for those just starting their careers it offers a picture of the types of positions that encompass this field.

Helping the Industry Help Itself

1

If corporations do not pay security employees at a competitive level, they will not get the best people. In general, corporations need to make sure that they are paying market rates in order to attract quality people, but budget issues require that they do not pay more than necessary. Personnel strategies vary widely from company to company, whether the company is willing to pay top dollar for employees who are the best in their field or prefer to hire less-qualified candidates at a lower cost. In every situation, solid information about security careers is a useful tool.

This book offers something for anyone responsible or interested in security careers.

It is a tool for **the entire corporation**—including the human resources and compensation departments, hiring manager, facility managers and executives, as well as the security department. The book can help to ensure that companies get the quality candidates they want, and that employees are paid a fair-market rate, or at least have a realistic expectation of what that rate is.

The book can help **individuals** manage their own careers and plan their next career moves. It is a great reference for anyone contemplating a career in corporate security, whether that person is leaving the government, military, or another business, or is early in his or her career or near retirement.

The book can be a resource for **career counselors** in the military and law enforcement fields, the source of many candidates for security jobs. All of these groups need access to a definitive source on the security career market. Now they have one. The candidate can now be just as informed as the interviewer. If everyone is on the same page, the right thing will happen, which often means that salaries will increase.

This book has been created for hands-on use. Readers may copy job descriptions and use them in hiring and staffing plans. They may share information on the many security organizations and trade publications with staff.

When credible career data is available for the security marketplace, suddenly every decision can be based on the real numbers determined by supply and demand. For more than 50 years, these numbers did not exist in the security market, except for occasional surveys by magazines or associations that sometimes underestimated pay levels because they did not have all the data. The job descriptions and salary levels described in this book provide "baseline" information. Of course, every job description and every salary level is subjected to "internal equity," that is, the expectation that the security professionals be paid comparably to other departments.

What the industry has needed, and now has in this book, is solid information based on accurate job descriptions and surveys of industry compensation professionals. Previously a lack of standardization often meant that security professionals were underpaid compared to employees in other departments with an equal level of responsibility in a company. Too often in the past, compensation departments and companies in general did not understand security jobs—it's a subject that is not often taught in business school. Security even tended to speak a different language than corporate executives, a language fraught with jargon borrowed from the military and law enforcement fields. Along with standardization, we can now also speak the same language.

The book can be a great planning document for managers in security departments everywhere. Its sample job descriptions can be used for reference to formulate descriptions specific to a company's needs.

There are three main purposes of this book:

1. **To standardize job descriptions so that they don't have to be rewritten by each company, and to collect them in one place for easy reference.** When job requirements are accurately documented, oftentimes positions need to be upgraded to reflect reality. Without accurate documentation, the true value of security jobs is not understood and too often not properly valued.

2. **To shed light on compensation practices and show security executives how they can influence them.** Historically, compensation professionals have not understood security or how security jobs fit into a company's broader hierarchy of positions. A security executive can use this book to help him or her communicate his or her department's needs to the compensation department, and do so in their language.

3. **To focus on certifications, qualifications, and other resources that can help security professionals manage their careers, and to know what they need to do to guide and facilitate their career path.** Beyond serving as a career self-counseling tool, the book can also be used for staff development and succession planning, and in college/university placement offices (where a book describing jobs in the security industry did not previously exist).

Our overarching goal should be to boost professionalism through education and expectation for given security roles. We are still an industry; what we need to do is become a profession. Using this book can provide a key element to get us there.

The Role and Responsibilities of the Security Leader

2

Many security leaders in the United States and around the world say that security today requires a range of skills that goes far beyond the capabilities of a traditional security director. In addition to law enforcement and military skills, a security leader must understand his or her firm's business, from finance and strategy to business continuity, competition, and profits. The security leader must employ executive leadership skills appropriate to the corporation as a whole. He or she must be able to communicate, manage large projects, create strategies, assemble cross-departmental teams, execute plans, and more.

A security leader must understand information technology (IT) security and must maintain an awareness of emerging issues that may affect the company. He or she must follow legislative and regulatory trends, developments in globalization, transnational crime, security research and development, and other trends that may one day alter the corporation's fortunes.

Today's most accomplished security leaders point to four general capabilities that define a modern security leader. First and foremost, a security head must understand his or her industry and company. Second, a security leader must develop a skill set that blends security, IT, business acumen, and the ability to identify and evaluate emerging issues. Third, a security leader must change with the time and grow with his or her company. Finally, he or she must possess an imagination capable of exploring for opportunities that will add value to the company.

Compare yourself against the security leader of the future

The following self-assessment tool lists 65 knowledge elements that can enhance the success of a security leader today. The skills fall under six general "knowledge streams" that produce six different kinds of values for businesses.

Law enforcement and military backgrounds, for example, provide knowledge of investigations and prosecutions. IT security skills help in the protection of critical information in both digital and printed formats. Business backgrounds help to align security value and business goals. A background career in corporate security ensures a security leader's intimate knowledge of a company. Executive leadership skills produce a focus on business results. Awareness of emerging issues helps to maintain situational readiness.

Table 2.1 Next Generation Security Leadership

Emerging and Horizon Issue Awareness	Business Elements	Executive Leadership Skills	IT Security Elements	Security Organization Elements	Government Elements
Value: Internal and External Situational Readiness	*Value: Alignment with Business*	*Value: Business results and Leadership*	*Value: Critical Information Protection*	*Value: Intimate Knowledge of the Particular Company/Business*	*Value: Risk Assessment & Mitigation*
Laws and regulatory trends	Finance	Communication skills	Network security	Knowledge of the business	Law enforcement
Cross-sector benchmarking	Sector/Industry-specific knowledge	Presentation skills	Computer/Platforms security	Corporate culture	Criminal justice system
Globalization developments	Business strategy	Project management	Applications	Internal processes	Investigations
Terrorism	Customer relations	Organization	Data and privacy protection	Employee familiarity	Physical security systems
Transnational crime	Organizational growth	Business acumen	IT policy	Institutional memory	Intelligence
Intellectual property protection	Business/Employee law	Strategic planning	System integration	Customers and issues	Counter intelligence
Outsourcing offshore	Business conduct and ethics	Relationship management	Operations continuity	Strategic alliances	Laws and ordinances
Gray Market/Counterfeiting	Business continuity	International experience	Data forensics	Brand/Reputation risk issues	Command and control
Security R&D	Business value measures/metrics	Team building	Data integrity investigations	Asset protection	Leadership training
	Competitive dynamics	Negotiation skills		Supply chain protection	Public sector access
	Profit and loss (P&L)	Decision skills		Incident response	Information protection
		Cost control		Crisis management	Emergency preparedness/response
				Policy and awareness	

Rate each element as: E=Expert, A=Adequate, I=Needs Improvement, M=Missing, or N/A=Not applicable to my situation or industry.

How well do you and your staff stack up to the security leader of the future? Evaluate yourself against each of the skills noted in Table 2.1. Assign a rating for each of the skills as follows:

E = Expert. These are skills you already possess.

A = Adequate. These are skills you can brush up on pretty quickly.

I = Needs improvement. These are skills you know you could improve upon.

M = Missing. These are skills you have no experience with and know nothing about.

N/A = Not applicable. These are skills that are not applicable to your particular situation or industry.

For each "E" rating you assign for a skill, give yourself three points. For each "A" rating you assign, give yourself two points. Give yourself one point for each "I" rating, and no points for either an "M" or "N/A" rating. When you finish, count up your points. Give yourself an additional one point up to a maximum of five points for every year of experience you have in one of the following fields: law enforcement, IT, business, and security.

Next, divide your score by two to get your "Next Generation" score. Those scoring 90 to 100 points can consider themselves ready to take on the challenges of twenty-first century security. A score from 80 to 89 points limits the role and level of your position in the organization. If you scored below 80, you may be risking your future. You should take steps now to expand your range of skills.

The history of the security role and a shift in the skills required

Government experience

History

Many security professionals have some form of government background, such as military or law enforcement experience. Chances are that background has served them well up to this point, but they may now find their career growth stagnating in the face of new requirements for high-level security positions.

Military experience was a staple of security hiring requirements as far back as the 1950s, when businesses saw the advantage in bringing the military know-how of servicemen returning from World War II into their security organizations. Before long, private corporations began to adopt physical security requirements that were similar to those of government entities, opening the door even further for those with military experience to step into security positions. The Cold War may have also fed business' interest in the military background. Emergency preparedness and rapid response took center stage, and these concerns remained important into the 1960s as businesses dealt with demonstrations and protests for civil rights and against the Vietnam War.

Organizations predominantly hired individuals with a military background for 10 to 15 years. Then, in the late 1970s and early 1980s, many began to focus instead on a background in law enforcement. Contracting and outsourcing had gained popularity in many business models in that time; the new employee was no longer necessarily someone known and trusted, but a potential risk. Companies were experiencing more internal theft and had more need for investigations, and instead of waiting on public law enforcement for help—an often fruitless endeavor—they began to hire ex-law enforcement officers who already had the knowledge they needed to root out the internal problems.

Strengths and drawbacks to the organization

The influx of military and law enforcement knowledge into security provided several advantages for businesses and the security industry. At the same time, it had some lasting negative impacts.

Advantages

- Those with government backgrounds already know the language of security, including standards and regulations.
- They know the tools of physical security, like cameras, access systems, and information security systems.
- They are well prepared to deal with certain challenges, such as civil insurrection.
- They maintain a strong focus on external threats.
- Law enforcement knows how to plan and conduct investigations.
- They know how to handle evidence.
- They are comfortable in the judicial process.
- They provide a needed response to growing internal threat.

Possible pitfalls

- Developing and maintaining the extensive physical security programs often proposed by former government professionals may be very expensive for private business, because relying on military knowledge alone often leads to an over-reliance on standards. Organizations may secure to standards instead of securing against risks that are specific to their business and location, which often leads to unnecessary cost.
- Neither approach stresses the involvement of every employee in corporate security. Unlike fire protection and life safety programs, security programs don't require staff to counsel employees on their roles in security, and management is not assigned responsibility either.
- There is often a clash between the corporate culture, processes, and behaviors, and the culture of law enforcement and military security to which the security professionals are accustomed.

The value of government knowledge today

Clearly the government skill set retains great value for security. Emergency preparedness, rapid response, risk assessment, and mitigation all remain fundamental elements of enterprise security. An understanding of physical security elements and processes will also always be a requirement of a well-rounded security program, no matter how the world changes. Physical protection of employees and assets remains a necessity for businesses, safeguarding not only their profits but also their reputations. And the need for in-house investigative skills has likely only increased with the advent of the new federal and industrial regulations of the past decade.

Transitioning to the next generation

There are, however, challenges for many security professionals attempting to expand their law enforcement or military skill sets to meet the needs of today's business-oriented security program. Three challenges stand out for security professionals hoping to transition from this background to a broader context.

1. **Regulation and Legislation.** New laws and regulations outline detailed physical security requirements that are tailored to certain types of organizations and market sectors, such as banks, hospitals, ports, and government facilities. However, it is becoming increasingly difficult to untangle physical regulations from other aspects, for example, information and business requirements. The complexity and frequency of investigations are also impacted by the glut of new laws.
2. **Technology.** The reach and capability of physical security systems and components has blossomed. Data on alarms and system performance is more centralized and accessible; video quality and affordability has increased remarkably; access control can be situated just about anywhere and can incorporate several levels of security. On the law enforcement side, investigations and prosecutions have been significantly complicated by the ubiquity of electronic data; IT expertise is increasingly important in investigations of misconduct and fraud that's based on data that may have been wiped from employee hard drives.
3. **Convergence.** Over the past 10 years or so, it may have seemed as though physical security would permanently lose out to information security, but the recent rash of high-profile laptop thefts have proven that physical security must be in place for information security to be effective. That said, the increasing inclusion of networked components in physical security systems does require a growing familiarity or comfort with IT concepts.

The most transferable skills

Luckily, there are a number of major skills that, while not unaffected by the challenges listed above, do align with today's business landscape.

Emergency preparedness/response

Businesses and public entities have increased their demand for emergency preparedness and response skills since September 11, 2001. These skills include risk and vulnerability assessment and planning, program development, training, information dissemination, development and management of drills and exercises, mass notification and casualty management, and evaluation of safety and security needs postevent.

Physical security systems

Events occur everyday to remind businesses of the continued importance of physical security knowledge, and their awareness is only heightened with the increasing convergence of physical and information security. Physical security skills include keeping abreast of available technologies, codes and legal requirements, managing in-house security technicians or overseeing third-party installers, risk and vulnerability assessment, and system design and planning.

Standards and regulations

The list of laws, regulations, and voluntary guidelines affecting security in all sectors is longer than you may know. Dealing with these requires a strong understanding of the security program and the business, authority within the organization, knowledge of all applicable regulations and guidelines, an understanding of your market sector and industry, and an understanding of legal and business ramifications.

Leadership training

Maintaining a successful security program means creating leaders at multiple levels of the organization. Leadership training calls for strong communication and interpersonal skills, knowledge of the organization, ability to motivate others, being a strong leader oneself, strong decision making, management, and team building.

Investigations

Probing the underbelly of the organization to find internal frauds and thieves has, arguably, never been more important. Strong investigations require interviewing skills, fact finding, information gathering, impartiality, knowledge of the organization and employees, awareness of privacy requirements, and understanding of legal limits and allowances.

Criminal justice system

Once investigations are complete, the security professional must know how to assist in effectively prosecuting the wrongdoers. Knowledge of the justice system and its requirements helps the security professional provide appropriate, strong testimony and correct handling and presentation of evidence.

Organizational experience

History

Individuals with government backgrounds held a monopoly on security positions throughout the 1970s because businesses wanted their knowledge of physical security, criminal justice, and investigation. But in the 1980s, that began to change. For 20 years, many organizations had experienced a growing culture clash with their government-trained security leaders, who often adopted a "my way or the highway" attitude in managing their departments and in communicating with other business units and executives.

Corporations began looking for security leaders who knew and understood their company's culture and could work within it instead of trying to force it into submission. They wanted new blood with an understanding of their internal processes, a familiarity with their employees, institutional memory, and knowledge of the brand, customers and business. Where better to look than in the organization itself? Management saw value in promoting security executives either from within the security department or from elsewhere within the business.

Business changes in this time period also factored into the increased focus on internal hiring. Companies were pushing to get 50% of their sales from international markets, globalizing the internal force, so through the mid-1990s managers expanded the hiring trend to focus on internal candidates with more international and intelligence experience.

Strengths and drawbacks

Leaders promoted from inside the organization had certain advantages that helped them effectively manage security.

They could work within the organization more easily. Internal leaders were able to shift the focus of the security management position from enforcing to enabling. Because they already knew the other executives in the business and understood how the business worked, they had an easier time partnering with other units than their predecessors from government backgrounds, who tended to push their agenda through instead of working with others to gain support. It also helped that businesses in the 1980s were beginning to encourage the formation of cross-functional teams for significant projects.

They were able to anticipate new security concerns dealing with asset protection and supply chain management. In the 1980s, when internal hiring was beginning to pick up steam, businesses began to change in another way. Distribution channels shifted away from warehouses to satellites and distribution centers. This drastically impacted business risks and protection needs, and internally promoted security leaders were able to recognize these impacts quickly because they understood how the business had been running before the shift. Leaders hired from outside would have had a much harder time picking up on the need for security to change with the business in this area.

They also suffered some significant disadvantages that complicated their tenure.

They often had little expertise in physical security, investigations, or criminal justice. In hiring from inside the organization, management got what they wanted: a partner and enabler who knew their business. However, they did not consider the extremely important skill sets they had lost from the government background. Instead of adding knowledge of the organization to the job description they already had, they often scrapped the old requirements entirely, which meant many new candidates had no knowledge of physical security, investigations, or criminal justice. Unfortunately, the need for these skills was every bit as important in the 1980s and 1990s as it had been in the decades before.

This meant that new internal leaders had to either hire their physical security and investigations experience or learn it themselves, taking precious time and attention away from the immediate protection of the enterprise.

Challenges transitioning

As those hired specifically for their internal experience work to move to the next generation of security leadership, they will experience some challenges. Chief among these is the potential for being blindsided by new trends. These individuals may focus on the organization to the exclusion of other things. They may also spend so much time trying to get the physical security and investigations knowledge under their belt that they forget to tune into management's changing needs and goals for the department. By taking their eyes off future trends, they may miss important business or industry turnings that significantly impact security.

Most transferable skills

Focus on the business. Businesses and industries are now so complex that you often have to be from the industry or company to understand what's going on. In the 1960s and 1970s, security leaders could get into any industry, because they all did things the same way—it was the same job at every company. In our data-centric society today, business changes accelerate so rapidly that it is difficult to keep up with new information unless you have come up through the business in that sector or vertical market.

Focus on partnership. In the next generation of security, the ability and will to partner with other business functions will continue to grow in importance. Individuals who have already cultivated this skill will have an advantage over those who have not.

IT experience

History

Information protection has been around since sensitive information was first put on paper. It resided mainly in government agencies and revolved mostly around internal movement. That is, files would move about within the organization, but were rarely intentionally passed to external sources. Documents moved by courier and were stored in filing cabinets, and securing them was a matter of watermarking and carefully controlling access.

With the advent and growing popularity of the Internet in the mid-1990s, information protection changed quickly and dramatically. Businesses were already creating and storing digital data, but suddenly these digital information assets could be moved within or outside the organization within seconds. IT security grew to include the protection of files, networks, databases, transactions, applications, and much more.

The increased business and consumer use of the Internet led to increased online attacks, which helped to grow the influence of and management support for IT security. A few high-profile attacks—such as the Code Red worm that infected 250,000 systems in just 9 h on July 19, 2001—raised IT security to even greater prominence.

In many organizations, IT security grew into its own entity outside the security department. This happened in part because the security leaders of the time, who had been promoted through the organization as discussed in last month's column, were in many cases caught off guard by the business shift to IT. Many of these leaders were so focused on gaining the security knowledge they lacked that this new vulnerability developed without their notice, until suddenly it became so large that it could not be ignored. By then, the IT organization had created its own security positions–positions that in some businesses eventually outranked the security director to become the leading security offices in the organization.

Strengths and drawbacks

Those with IT security backgrounds brought valuable knowledge to their organizations.

- **They knew the systems, applications, and platforms the business needed to perform at its peak in the information age.** They knew or knew how to discover the vulnerabilities of these systems, applications, and platforms, and they knew how to shore them up. Basically, they enabled the business to safely expand into the world of the Web.
- **They enabled regulatory compliance.** The information security requirements of SOx and the Federal Sentencing Guidelines gave IT security a leading role in compliance. Their knowledge of the solutions in place and available helped the business comply more quickly, avoiding fines.
- **They created a large body of standards and repeatable processes** that enhanced IT security across organizations.

IT security professionals also brought some limitations to the leading security role. Chief among these:

- **They did not enforce punishment for cyber crime.** Because IT security professionals did not have any background in law enforcement or investigation, they did not work to stop cyber criminals from exploiting their networks. Instead, they focused their attention on patching up the system once the damage was done. This held true in the vast majority of the IT community, and it led to a preponderance of cyber crime that was almost social in nature because criminals did not fear prosecution.
- **There was a perception that IT culture did not mesh with corporate culture.** While many IT security professionals interacted regularly with other departments, other executives often observed their high-tech language and unfamiliar solutions and equated these with arrogance or standoffishness. That said, certain types of positions often do attract certain types of personality, and the IT personality is not always team oriented. In fact, communication was not a priority for some IT folks, and these created their own space in the organization and did not often venture out to work with other units.

Challenges transitioning

This cultural issue continues to be a stumbling block for many IT security leaders who look to move to the next generation, although by the time they have gained executive status, many IT professionals have vastly improved their communication with other departments. However, another communication problem remains. IT professionals often speak in code, discussing security issues in a very specific technical language that other executives may have trouble understanding. This can complicate collaboration.

IT security professionals may also struggle to show the business value of their contribution and may have a hard time communicating how some technologies can save the business money.

Most transferable skills

Of course, the IT professional's technical knowledge and innovation will be key to securing the business of the future. As more business communication goes wireless and handheld, IT security expertise will become even more important. And since online and digital business applications will likely only grow in acceptance, innovation in IT security will serve the business well.

Executive leadership experience

History

In the 1980s and 1990s, companies began encouraging or requiring their employees and managers in all sectors, including security, to bone up on executive leadership skills, such as the ability to manage large budgets, to negotiate, influence peers, coordinate external initiatives, lead staff, and communicate and present effectively. Corporations held internal training courses and seminars and more tightly incorporated the use of leadership skills into many of their internal functions.

Three main factors contributed to companies' increased interest in these skills: international competition, quality initiatives, and technology.

In the 1980s it became clear that foreign competitors were outperforming U.S. companies in several big markets, including auto manufacturing and technology. Imports from Japan and Germany were taking domestic business from U.S. corporations, and business leaders wanted to know why.

Their answer was quality. U.S. products and customer service were simply below par. Foreign competitors had espoused widespread use of management philosophies like statistical process control to ensure that defects rarely reached their customers, while U.S. companies continued to rely on more traditional methods.

In response to this finding, U.S. corporations launched into a frenzy of quality initiatives. Six Sigma, Total Quality Management, Tom Peters' *In Search of Excellence*—corporations pushed these teachings out to every staffer in every function, and their impact was inescapable.

At the same time, organizations were prepping their employees to deal with international business abroad in order to better compete overseas. Companies wanted to drastically improve their standing in international sales, yet stories abounded of executives going to China and Japan and committing cultural suicide—insulting their hosts or potential customers because they did not know anything about the customs and traditions of the countries. Organizations began to train employees on cultural issues and public speaking so they could present a better face for the company internationally.

Technology also played a role in the focus on executive leadership skills. For one thing, technology was in part responsible for the increase in international competition and the growth of the global marketplace. But it also required employees to learn new skills. When e-mail became widespread in the workplace, corporations often held classes on how to communicate appropriately in this new medium and how to avoid abusing this tool in their management activities.

As the 2000s neared, companies cut down or eliminated their internal training for executive leadership skills due to cost.

Most transferable skills

All of the skills in the executive leadership skill set—presentation skills, strong communication, building peer influence, managing large budgets—are immediately valuable to the security professional hoping to excel or to reach a C-level seat, and they are also valuable once that goal is attained. Internal training for these skills was not eliminated because they had declined in importance, but because they had become an expectation rather than a posthiring issue. These skills are now routinely included in job descriptions and hiring requirements, so security professionals that do not have them may not be able to compete as well in the job market. Many security professionals already have several skills in this set, such as negotiation skills, team building, decision-making skills, and relationship management.

Challenges transitioning

One of the most difficult aspects of gaining executive leadership skills, particularly for those new to the workforce or the field, is finding a training program. When these skills were being taught inside the organization, security got to participate in in-house training with everybody else. Now, professionals have to bear the cost burden on their own by enrolling in training courses offered by specialty organizations or colleges. Some external training courses that claim to be tailored for security do not actually provide much useful knowledge specifically for the security professional.

This problem also exists within organizations where security professionals were trained with the rest of the staff. The in-house training provided by companies in the 1980s and 1990s was not customized for security, and often the security department did not do enough to update the training for their own purposes. Because security has a unique perspective and unique responsibilities within the organization, it was difficult for the security department to customize the messages of executive leadership to their own environment.

Business experience

So far we have focused on individual elements of successful security leadership, looking at each skill set in the context of the specific time period in which management homed in on it as a requirement for security professionals. Roughly each decade since the 1950s, management has focused in on one new skill set as the silver bullet for security or the business. Some hiring managers focused on these new skill sets to the exclusion of other skills that were equally important to the well-rounded security leader's portfolio, while many senior managers instead simply added the new skill sets to their list of qualifications for security leadership.

A few years ago, all the skill sets we have previously discussed—the skills that come from government or military experience, the ability to know and work within the organization, IT security knowledge, and executive leadership skills—were considered baseline skills that senior management simply expected to see in security directors and CSOs. Then, in 2003 and 2004, yet another set was added to the pile. Management began looking for business skills, such as aligning the department with the overall business goals and adding value to the company, from all its leaders, including those in security. In some organizations, this new responsibility is stretching already strapped security departments to their limits.

History

In 2003 and 2004, extreme competition and Wall Street pressure were taking their toll on corporations and their shareholders. Companies had tried everything to add revenue—cut costs, increased quality, improved customer service—but every time one company made an innovative breakthrough in one business area, every other company emulated it, taking away any competitive advantage.

Having exhausted their other options, organizations turned to their business units and asked them to find ways to add value from within. If a department was considering a new service or technology product, the purchase could only be justified through a statement of how it could add value to the corporation.

Even in areas like security and IT, which had traditionally been driven by the latest and greatest in technology, new technology had to be scrutinized under the lens of corporate value. Nicholas Carr's book *Does IT Matter*, published in 2004, introduced the idea that IT had become a commodity rather than a competitive advantage, and whichever company could achieve IT goals effectively at the lowest cost would benefit the most.

Security faced a similar shift. Technology like CCTV and even digital or IP cameras, whose prices were already rapidly dropping, had become commonplace in security programs. Management now wanted more from these investments. Instead of using cameras for surveillance alone, companies wanted to see them shared with marketing departments to determine the effectiveness of sales displays, or with quality control to view the production floor.

Opportunities for security

At this same time, brand reputation and corporate image had skyrocketed in value. Company after company succumbed to scandal and the loss of customers that accompanied it, and they served as an example to all others to protect the brand ferociously.

Security has an advantage here. Many of security's basic responsibilities play a natural role in protecting the brand. For example, student safety and security are extremely valuable to universities, not only for ethical and compliance reasons but also because safety is a reputational issue. Campus shootings like those at Northern Illinois University and Virginia Tech make some parents think twice about enrolling their sons and daughters there. The school that can demonstrate safety and security can gain higher enrollment and community confidence.

Similarly, banks and retailers protect customer privacy online not only because of regulation, but because customer confidence in the security of their personal and financial information is valuable. Privacy breaches result in lost customers, so it is in a bank's or a retailer's best interest to make customers feel safe online.

Security is now a brand advantage in many markets, so adding value is easily within the reach of many security leaders.

The pitfalls of investment and presentation

Two major problems present themselves as security enters into the "value added" world, however.

While adding value with security may often seem like a no brainer, it is far from simple when the security program lacks all the resources it needs to do its job. Management's requirement for all business units to add value makes good business sense, but senior management often does not know anything about what it would take for the security program to accomplish that. They often do not recognize that in order to get value from security, they have to invest in the people and services needed to run security effectively. They also do not always recognize that there are limitations to what security can do. There is only so much security can do when dealing with international laws and cultural differences, for instance. Management may not understand why they cannot prosecute hackers from a foreign country.

Knowing that you are adding value is not the same as showing senior management how you are doing it. Many security professionals may have a strong sense of the company's goals and how security can contribute to them, but without a program to measure the effectiveness of security, they will not be able to make their case to management.

Be aware of emerging issues

Emerging issue awareness is perhaps the most difficult to define and the most difficult to obtain of all the knowledge areas the next generation security leader must master. It is not taught at universities or learned by mentoring, it means something different in every company and industry, and upper management is looking for it now more than ever.

The term "emerging issue awareness" does not appear in lists of job qualifications or requirements, but it is often there, hidden in other language. Where a job calls for a "strategic thinker", someone "able to anticipate", who is adept at "planning for current and future needs" and "meeting the needs of a changing business environment"—there it calls for the elements of emerging issue awareness.

Being aware of emerging issues affecting the security of the company means making sure your senior management is never caught by surprise. It means keeping tabs on happenings and changes within the company; its industry; the security industry; business in general; technology; crime; local, national and global politics and threats; and any other arena that could impact the organization.

This may sound like a lot to expect of the security executive, but to successfully provide security in today's business and economic environment, this skill set is a necessity. Threats can come at an organization from any angle or direction, and lack of preparation for them may cause extremely damaging financial, reputational, and safety issues.

In an unpublished interview with the Security Executive Council in 2008, Dick Lefler, former CSO of American Express, member of the executive board of advisors and dean of emeritus faculty of the Security Executive Council, pinpointed several historical examples that illustrate the wide range of emerging threats the next generation security leader must prepare for. On one hand, he noted the effects of 9/11 and Hurricane Katrina on companies that maintained current, tested business continuity and crisis response plans and those that did not. In these examples, the CSO who kept up with the best practices of the security industry and the potential impacts of terrorism or natural disasters was able to provide his or her company with a higher level of business protection and safety.

On the other hand, he highlighted a single, seemingly minor technology evolution: the development and improvement of the color copier. When this device improved to the point that reproductions were indistinguishable from the originals at first glance, it changed counterfeiting from a sophisticated crime that could only be perpetrated with specialized equipment, to something that could be done by anyone with a quick trip to Kinkos. "In this case," Lefler explained, "the CSO's familiarity with technology trends is what allows him or her to prepare countermeasures to meet an emerging threat."

The security leader's emerging issue awareness should encompass not only external concerns, but also changes within the corporation. If the business is getting ready to outsource, offshore, change packaging, or embark on joint ventures, mergers, or acquisitions, or even if there is a drop in sales, the security leader has to be aware of these potential changes. Then he or she must determine what those changes will mean to security and how best to respond.

Challenges to emerging issue awareness

Ten years ago, if we wanted information on the happenings in a certain area, company, or industry, we often had to scrounge to find it. Now we are buried in it. The Internet presents an overwhelming amount of information to the security leader searching for issues that may impact his or her company.

Maintaining constant watch over such a wide variety of potential risks and threats in a constant flood of data is a challenge that can be overcome through discipline and organization, as we will discuss below. But recognizing within that sea of information which issues constitute emerging risks is a matter of experience combined with aptitude. Unlike some of the other knowledge areas we have discussed in this series, emerging issue awareness cannot be learned through academic programs, books, or other sources of training. It requires the security leader to train himself or herself over time to quickly identify significant issues as they develop.

Tips for staying aware

There are myriad sources of information you can monitor to keep watch for issues that may impact your company. Industry associations, corporate public relations and investor relations departments, magazines, television stations and newspapers, government organizations, and research groups all offer services that help keep you up to date on the events that matter to them, in the form of e-newsletters, RSS feeds, news services, blogs, and Web sites.

The security leader's first challenge is to choose the right sources. Knowing your business and your security program, as well as your industry and the regions in which your company operates, will be crucial to choosing well. Sometimes this also requires creative thinking. In the same interview mentioned earlier, Lefler explained that sometimes the best way to forecast and prepare for threat trends is to keep an eye on other industries that do not seem to have much to do with your own.

For instance, he said, if you are in pharmaceuticals and you anticipate problems with counterfeiting, you can learn something by watching how luxury goods manufacturers deal with their counterfeiting problems, then picking out the elements of their solutions that would be useful in your context. Similarly, if your company puts you in charge of protecting two million acres of timber and you find you have a timber theft problem, you can look to unmanned aircraft technology developed by the military for defense purposes to help you patrol the company's property. "Part of the chief security officer's (CSO) job," said Lefler, "is to understand how to bring cost-effective solutions to emerging threats by looking at what's going on in other sectors and converting that to your own thinking."

Once you have chosen relevant sources of information and subscribed to their services, the next challenge is sorting through all the e-mails, feeds, sites, and mailings to find the news that is meaningful for you and then to identify patterns and interpret the trends you see. It is important to remember that each source has a different slant on the news they provide.

If you want to avoid buckling under the weight of all this information, you must develop good habits and practice constant self-discipline. Here are some tips for handling the information overload.

- **Scan everything.** Learn to glance through magazine, e-news, and newspaper headlines and to get the gist of the story without stopping to read every word. Speed reading courses can bring real value.
- **Consolidate.** Avoid single-source documents or mailings; focus instead on news scanners, which pick out headlines based on criteria you set and only send you information that might be useful to you.
- **Organize.** Keep a separate e-mail folder for group mailings so that these items do not clog up your regular inbox. But set aside time every morning to scan through the folder and clear it out. Don't let it pile up.
- **Ask for help.** If you do not think you can do all this sorting and organizing by yourself, appoint a staff member to help you cull through the information. Another option is to partner with an analyst group that searches news based on your criteria and notifies you about items that are actionable or critical.
- **Network.** In your profession and across sectors, be prepared to be a fast follower on new ideas and solutions.

Managing Compensation: Factors that Influence Compensation Decisions

3

Welcome to the world of compensation, a subject that affects all executives, managers, and employees. The material has been written in user-friendly terms so that you can address the topic of compensation intelligently without being overwhelmed by details. This chapter is not intended for the professional human resource and compensation practitioner who is educated and trained in the subject of compensation administration. It is directed toward the security manager, who often finds himself or herself thrust into the often challenging and sometimes complex process of administering a compensation program to attract, retain, motivate, and reward employees.

Typically, you are not concentrating on issues of compensation administration while you are developing your area of expertise as a manager. Our intent is to provide the reader with a general summary of some of the influences that drive decisions in compensation, for example, hiring rates, competitive practices for specific jobs and grade placement. Also provided are the tools to formulate a recommendation on compensation as it applies to your employees and give you the knowledge to defend those decisions.

You will be introduced to the major components of a compensation program and how they are developed. We will explain how the organization's compensation philosophy affects your decisions and approaches to managing your employees' pay. We will explain the fundamentals of developing a base wage and salary program using job descriptions, internal ranking of positions, and how to evaluate those positions for internal and external value. To help you work most effectively with your Human Resources and Compensation Department we will help you understand the "compensation lingo" often used by these professionals. There are various types of compensation surveys; you will learn which type works best for you and how to understand and use the information. We will even cover the methodology and processes for developing and administering your wage and salary budget.

Compensation philosophy of the organization

Most organizations have a defined compensation philosophy that applies to all employees. This philosophy will determine where the company targets its compensation elements, such as base pay, cash bonus, long-term incentives, and employee benefits. A compensation philosophy is typically a comprehensive statement of how the organization structures its overall compensation program in relationship to competitors and the current labor market. For example, the company might target its pay levels to the average, the median or the 75th percentile of competitive levels. Most companies establish a wage and salary grade structure to accommodate their targeted compensation position in the marketplace. The compensation philosophy is directly linked to the overall business goals and objectives of the company and is translated into a defined pay program detailing all the components to ensure that the organization will be able to attract, retain, motivate, and reward top talent for each position.

Traditionally, various employee groups within an organization require specifically designed approaches to pay programs to meet overall business goals and objectives. In other words, there may be multiple approaches in program design based on various groups of positions within an organization, but still meet the stated compensation philosophy guidelines. For example, an organization that perceives the sales function as critical in achieving overall financial success might target the sales staff's base pay below the stated guideline, but target the incentive component well above the guideline.

Definition of wage and salary programs

Two basic classifications of wage and salary programs have arisen from legislation known as the Federal Fair Labor Standards Act (FLSA). One FLSA classification covers "non-exempt" employees, requiring this group be paid overtime for any time worked more than 8 h per day or 40 h per week. Nonexempt employees are generally paid an hourly wage on a weekly basis. The other classification covers "salaried" employees who are "exempt" from the terms of FLSA. Exempt (or salaried) employees do not receive pay for overtime hours and are usually paid semimonthly or monthly. The company's compensation group is responsible for placing all positions into the appropriate category based on current FLSA interpretations.

Components of compensation

A mix of various pay elements that a given individual within a position can potentially earn are combined to make up the total compensation package. Various compensation components are in addition to the base wage and salary. The more common of these additional components of compensation include the following.

Cash bonus

A cash payment to reward employees when the organization meets or exceeds its financial and/or specific performance goals. Bonuses are generally a variable part of the pay program and not guaranteed. They are normally paid quarterly or annually,

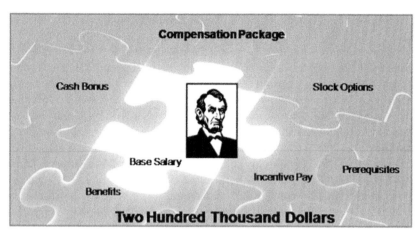

FIGURE 3.1

Compensation Components.

typically in cycle with the organization's fiscal year. Bonuses are usually designed as a percentage of base pay and include cash profit-sharing programs.

Short-term incentive pay

Various forms of monetary payment used to motivate and reward employees for individual and/or organization performance. Incentives are generally not guaranteed and are a variable part of the pay program. An incentive program is designed to focus on an employee's goals and objectives based on defined results within a specific time. Incentives are paid out monthly, quarterly, or annually. The incentive "carrot" is typically designed to encourage an employee to focus on specific personal and organization goals and objectives, such as meeting expense budget objectives or a sales quota.

Long-term incentive

Any variable pay components paid out more than one year from the start of the program. Long-term incentives are typically some form of deferred payment that is paid out in cash and/or company stock. These programs are usually based on long-term financial and performance goals over a specific number of years established by the organization.

Stock option grants

The issuance of unrestricted common shares of a company's stock to an employee. Stock options allow employees to purchase company stock at a fixed price (strike price) at the time of the grant on a specific vesting schedule. Vesting will occur over a specified time (varying by company from monthly to annually). The stock plan has defined exercise dates (the dates an employee can buy and/or sell the stock). For example, say an employee is granted 1000 shares of company stock on January 1, 2013. The stock price on January 1, 2013 is $10. The program has a four-year vesting cycle of 25% per year over the life of the stock option grant. This means the employee has control of buying and selling 250 shares each year over a four-year period ($250 \times 4 = 1000$ shares). On January 1, 2014, the employee has vested in 250 shares, and the stock is now selling at $12 per share. The difference between the grant price of $10 and the current market value of $12 is a gain of $2 per share. If an employee sells their 250 shares on January 1, 2014, they would receive $500 before taxes. If on January 1, 2014 the stock price is $6, the stock is considered "underwater." The price of the stock at the time of grant is more than the fair market value at the time the shares are vested. At the end of four years, the employee is fully vested in the stock grant and can exercise all the shares. Once vested, employees do not have to sell their shares until a predetermined "end" date, usually 10 years or termination of employment. Typically, positions eligible for option grants receive them annually during the performance review cycle.

Restricted stock grants

Also known as letter stock or restricted securities, these refer to stock of a company that is not fully transferable until certain conditions have been met. Upon satisfaction of those conditions, the stock becomes transferable by the person holding the grant. Another type of restricted stock is a form of compensation granted by a company. Typically, the conditions allow the shares to be transferred when they are vested. However, those restrictions can also be some sort of performance condition, such as the company reaching earnings per share goals or financial targets. Restricted stock is becoming a more prominent form of employee compensation, particularly to executives.

Benefits

Including such items as life insurance, medical-dental insurance, long-term disability plans, retirement plans (pension and/or 401K programs), profit-sharing plans, paid vacation, and sick leave programs.

Perquisites

Perquisites (or "perks," as they are informally referred to) are usually granted as tangible items, such as a company car. Other forms of perquisites may include a country club membership, first class air travel, company parking space, home mortgage assistance, or utilization of the corporate airplane. Typically, perquisites are granted based on position requirements, e.g. field sales staff or senior level positions within the organization.

The role of the compensation group

In most cases, the compensation group is part of the human resources function within an organization, and their direct reporting relationship is to the Human Resources Department. The compensation staff is charged with the responsibility of ensuring that the compensation philosophy is administered equitably throughout the organization. This is achieved by working with line and staff management to develop competitive hiring rates, wage and salary grade structures, career ladders, merit increase plans and schedules, cash bonus plans, short-term and long-term incentives, and benefit programs and perquisites. Equally important, the compensation group is responsible for supporting their assigned organizational group (or groups) within the company. Having direct support from a compensation specialist ensures internal equity and external compensation competitiveness. The compensation specialist can be most effective when working closely with security managers. An important role for the compensation staff is to coach, guide, and support management in the area of compensation administration.

Base wage and salary programs

Companies use two types of pay programs to analyze internal and external value of positions: the widely used pay program called "Whole Job Ranking—Market Pricing," and a second methodology called "Point Factor—Market Pricing."

Whole job ranking

The "whole job ranking" process compares each position horizontally and vertically within the security unit and throughout the company. The approach is flexible and fairly easy to administer.

Using the job descriptions developed by the compensation specialist and approved by the security manager, the two parties evaluate the internal value of each position by comparing the job description to similar jobs in the business unit. The internal value is based on position attributes such as job knowledge, education, and accountability as they are applied to the function of the job internally. This exercise establishes the internal value and a hierarchy of positions based solely on the unit's relative internal value. This is the "whole job ranking" portion of the base wage and salary program.

Once all managers in security function complete a hierarchy by ranking their positions internally, the next step is to compare all business units within the company to ensure position equity based on internal value. The process involves unit representatives ranking the jobs by reviewing placement by their peers for all jobs across the organizational structure. This exercise provides perspective to the internal value of each position and the perceived importance to the company's success. The compensation group can now begin to determine the external value of each position.

Market pricing

Generally, companies participate in compensation surveys to determine external value, or market competitiveness, of each position. The compensation group matches the company's current job descriptions and the internal hierarchy of positions to the survey positions.

The compensation specialist ensures the appropriate compensation survey is selected for a specific job family. He or she ascertains from security and compliance management what group of companies (same industry or multiple industries) they perceive would employ individuals in comparable positions requiring similar skills and qualifications. This step is critical to guaranteeing the validity of the data on which compensation decisions are based.

When the company chooses to participate in one or more salary surveys, the compensation group submits the necessary data. Numerous recognized compensation consulting firms regularly solicit the compensation group to participate in position and industry-specific surveys. Considering the company's needs, the compensation group identifies those surveys that best meet their requirements. Available information from a survey should be consistent with the company's compensation philosophy for market competitiveness for example, average, median, or 75th percentile. Positions that are reported in a survey and are a good match to the company's job description information will become "benchmark jobs" or jobs that can be market priced on an annual basis. It is important to note that comparing jobs in the survey should not be based on matching job titles; the only valid way to match the company's jobs to survey positions is by comparison of actual job content and requirements from the job descriptions.

Considering the market data, the compensation group creates a hierarchy of the same positions used for the internal analysis. Many positions will not change their ranking in their hierarchy based on market and internal equity. This is the "market pricing" portion of the pay program. The market may recognize a position to be of greater worth than the internal value placed on the position by the security management. In these cases, the compensation group reviews with the security manager the difference in the market hierarchy versus the value placed on the internal ranking. The manager may elect to recognize market influences and move the position in the internal hierarchy, or may recommend leaving the position where it was ranked based on internal value. If the manager elects to align the position with market, the position stays a benchmark job. If the position is moved from a market target or is chosen to stay at the internal value, then it is labeled a "non-benchmark job." This process also serves as a basis for developing a company's grade structure (discussed later in this chapter).

Point factor program

The second type of pay program companies use to develop the internal and external value of a position is called a "point factor pay program." This type of program would normally be developed by an outside compensation consultant specializing in such programs. Some of the mechanics are similar to a market pricing-whole job ranking program, but there are distinct differences. In a point factor approach, skill-sets are developed to reflect the specific and unique requirements to the organization, typically including job knowledge, problem solving, accountability, and other job content requirements determined by the organization. Each skill-set is given a point value with varying degrees applied to each skill. For example, the position under the skill "managerial job knowledge" will call for both management skill and basic technical knowledge. The skill assessments will have an X- and Y-axis and a point value will be assigned to each axis.

A compensation committee is formed, including representative managers from various organizational units in the company. The compensation consultants, along with the compensation group, would train the managers on job evaluation methodologies. Each job in the organization is formally evaluated using the point factor system. After evaluation, each position in the organization would have points associated with each factor, and a total point value would be assigned to the position. Each company's total point value for each position is different, because their job factor weighting is based on each organization's financial size and business complexity.

The consulting team would set the market price of the company's assigned total points for each position to the published survey data of market price. The compensation survey information would represent organizations in the same industry (industrial, financial, etc.) that uses the same or similar point factor approach. This approach limits the survey resources available and the flexibility of the salary administration program. Point factor systems have been widely embraced historically and are still in use by some companies today. However, due to the significant costs, time, and effort they take to develop and maintain, the point factor system has lost favor with many compensation professionals.

Compensation surveys

There are several types of compensation surveys for determining external position value. The most popular are categorized into three groups:

1. Third party compensation surveys
   a. Paid for by a requesting organization.
   b. Conducted by independent consulting and survey firms.
   c. Participating companies pay a fee to participate and receive the report.
2. Club compensation surveys
   a. Sponsored by a specific company.
   b. Conducted by independent consulting and survey firms.
   c. Invited only to select sample of peer and/or competitive companies.
3. Trade association compensation surveys
   a. Information obtained through association sources or association members input only.

FIGURE 3.2

Types and Advantages of Compensation Surveys.

From a compensation practitioner's view, compensation surveys are the cornerstone of a company's ability to assess market competitiveness. Compensation surveys gauge what the market is paying a particular position based on a set of descriptors that define the position. All jobs, from an entry-level job to the chief executive officer, have a defined value in the marketplace, and compensation surveys enable a multitude of companies to participate and then review what the market is willing to pay for a particular position.

The U.S. Department of Justice "Safe Harbor Guidelines"

The Department of Justice (DOJ) has specific guidelines for conducting compensation surveys, under the antitrust safety zones called "Safe Harbor Guidelines." These guidelines are designed to prevent companies from colluding in the marketplace to set wages and salaries. Safe Harbor Guidelines were developed in response to group of companies in the same industry directly sharing wage and salary data among themselves. The DOJ deems this practice collusion outside "free market forces" and considers it "price fixing" within an industry. For example, one of the components to meet "Safe Harbor Guidelines" in compensation survey reports is that no data should be included if the position data reflect less than five organizations and less than five employees.

Third party compensation surveys

These are surveys conducted by independent consulting and survey firms functioning as third parties to gather and publish compensation data. These surveys provide meaningful, reliable, confidential, and statistically sound information. Participating companies pay a fee to the survey firm to participate and receive the final data. The survey organization develops the survey product, invites appropriate companies to participate, collects compensation data, audits the information, and publishes the statistical data. Data are reported in the aggregate; no individual employee compensation within the company is identified. To ensure the validity of the reported information, the survey firm challenges any survey data submitted that appears to be inappropriate. These consulting and survey organizations work within the DOJ's "Safe Harbor Guidelines" and are totally objective when evaluating and reporting the information.

Generally, compensation survey reports include complete job descriptions and the company's degree of match to the survey descriptions. The data are reported in the aggregate displaying compensation information by percentile levels. In addition, data are reported by company revenue, geographic location, and type of industry. Participating companies are listed and the date the data was collected is included to enable participants to "age" the data, if necessary, during their analysis and application. Typically, third party surveys are conducted and produced annually, and participating companies may be involved in updating and submitting new positions to be surveyed.

Third party surveys are an economical way for a company to obtain current compensation information and protect themselves from "Safe Harbor" violations. This form of survey may be industry- and/or job-, and family-specific, depending on the needs of the company. An "industry-specific" survey, for example, the Energy Industry is one that focuses on and is designed just for, companies in that industry. A "job-family-specific" survey might be targeted to a range of businesses but might focus on a specific family of jobs, such as sales and marketing.

Club compensation surveys

A club compensation survey is usually one that is sponsored by a specific company and is designed to target a select sample of peer or competitive companies. This type of survey is similar to the third party approach explained above, except that it is sponsored by a single company. The survey is by invitation only, and the sponsoring company retains a third party compensation consulting and survey firm to conduct and produce the survey to meet the requirements of the "Safe Harbor Guidelines." The "club" comprises those companies that compete with one another and are usually specific to a certain industry, such as pharmaceutical or energy. Companies are willing to participate because most of the jobs are applicable to their industry and they receive the results free of charge. Invited firms submit salary, bonus, or other data the sponsoring company is seeking for each surveyed position. The survey firm, acting as a third party, develops the questionnaire, manages the response process, audits the data, distributes the survey results to participants, and briefs the sponsoring company on the final report.

Trade association compensation surveys

Trade association surveys report compensation information obtained through industry association survey sources or individual membership of the association. Most trade association surveys are conducted by the association itself, but sometimes they are produced by a third party firm. The results are typically free to association members. A survey questionnaire is developed and distributed to association members. Historically, compensation surveys conducted by trade associations have been questioned due to credibility issues. The Association members are asked to submit their own personal compensation information, which may appear to be self-serving, as opposed to the company staff submitting the specific pay data. This form of data prevents the survey administrator from validating the responses. Corporate compensation and human resources staff often hesitate to rely on this type of survey information because of perceived credibility issues.

Compensation survey participation

When considering whether to participate in a compensation survey, the security manager and the compensation specialist should ask the following key questions.

How many positions in the security organization unit match those in the survey?

There is no magic number; it is a matter of your need for specific information on positions critical to your unit. You may ask the survey firm to send position descriptions for review and to ascertain how many matches you may have to the survey.

What types of data are collected and what type of data does the security manager need for their organization?

Do you need information such as average base salary and bonus practices, or do you need specific information, such as hiring rates for recent college graduates?

What other companies are participating?

Some believe that they should participate in surveys that include only competitive companies. You should ask, "Do you only recruit from competitive companies?" The answer is typically, "No, we recruit from a wider market." So you should consider a more macroview of the market and seek information on compensation from surveys that include competitors and other companies seeking talent in the same market.

What is the cost of participating in the survey?

Survey costs are all over the board, from $250 to thousands of dollars. Some surveys require companies to participate to receive the results. Often, surveys may be purchased once by nonparticipants, and the survey firm requires the purchaser to participate the following year. If the company does not participate the following year, the survey firm may not let the company participate again. The question on cost is this: Can you afford not to know what the market is paying for your positions? If a survey costs $1000 and takes 3h to complete, it is a small investment compared to losing key employees due to compensation issues.

Has the human resources/compensation group bought into a specific compensation survey for security positions?

It is important that you communicate specific concerns and needs. If the budget is an issue for the human resources/compensation group, you may want to offer to pay for the survey out of your security unit's budget.

Survey statistics

Most surveys will include a section that defines the terms of the survey data. The following are a few of the most commonly used terms. (Chapter 4 provides examples of security-related job descriptions.)

Position title: The title used in the survey to identify the job. Participants should be cautious when using the position title as the sole reference in matching their positions to survey data. Organizations often report numerous titles for the same job content.

Job description: The generic description defining the nature, scope, and responsibilities of the position in the survey. The descriptions are usually developed from material gathered from participant organizations. The more comprehensive the job content and qualification guidelines in the descriptions, the more reliable the survey results are.

Minimum qualifications: Defines the minimum education and years of experience required to perform the job responsibilities in a competent manner.

Degree of position match: Participants are asked to match their position description to the job description presented in the survey and to indicate the degree of match (less than description, very close match, more than description) to provide the participant with a reference point when using the survey report. Participants should use the information from surveys with caution when position data indicates a higher percentage in the categories "less than" or "more than" position match.

Base salary (all employees): Annual base salary paid to all employees in the specific position, excluding any additional income (cash bonus, profit sharing, overtime, shift differentials, etc.).

Base salary (bonus eligible): Annual base salary to employees who are eligible for extra cash income.

Base salary (not bonus eligible): Annual base salary to employees who are not eligible for extra cash income.

Bonus amount (actual paid): Actual annual cash bonus amount reported for those employees paid a bonus. These are cash payments in addition to base wage or salary and are used to reward employees for company and/or individual performance. Bonuses are generally not guaranteed and are a variable part of the pay program.

Total cash compensation: Annual base salary plus the annual cash bonus or cash incentive paid, if any, for all employees in the classification. The total compensation figure represents all employees in the survey group, regardless of whether they were paid a cash bonus and incentive.

Total compensation (bonus eligible): Annual base salary plus cash bonus or cash incentive for only those employees receiving a bonus. These figures represent total cash compensation for only those employees in the survey group, regardless of whether they received a cash bonus or cash incentive.

Number of organizations: Total number of organizations reporting data for the position.

Number of employees: Total number of individual employees occupying and carrying out the job as described in the survey description.

Weighted average: The compensation weighted average is determined by the number of employees receiving a specific pay level. For each job, the weighted average is computed by multiplying each company's salary by their number of incumbents, adding these values and dividing by the total number of employees for each job.

10th percentile: Given an ordered array of data, 10% of the data falls below this value.

25th percentile: Given an ordered array of data, 25% of the data falls below this value (also known as the 1st Quartile rate).

Median: Given an ordered array of data, one-half of the employees are paid above this figure and one-half are paid below this figure (also known as the 50th Percentile).

75th percentile: Given an ordered array of data, 75% of the data falls below this value (also known as the 3rd Quartile rate).

90th percentile: Given an ordered array of data, 90% of the data falls below this value.

Average salary range: The average annual salary ranges of all participating organizations that have an established salary range structure. The salary range defines the established minimum, midpoint, and maximum range opportunity that an employee in the position can expect to be paid.

Depending on the survey, there may be other data points shown, such as eligibility for stock options and other extra income (bonus, profit sharing), etc. There may also be various breakouts of compensation data by geographic region, revenue, or type of industry.

The most important point to remember about surveys is that they are a snapshot in time of compensation market information. Compensation is a moving target, so if you want to stay current and competitive, you should give serious consideration to a scheduled participative role in reliable surveys.

Defining a "Benchmark Compensation Survey"

A "Benchmark Survey" is a term used by companies to identify the surveys they use on a consistent basis, either semiannually or annually. The positions in the survey are referred to as "benchmarks" because they are very good matches to the company's jobs. The position descriptions in the survey do not have to be jobs in the same industry as the participating company, but could represent a good cross-section of organizations with comparable positions.

Benchmark surveys are used for a company's salary planning, such as structure development, merit schedules, and career "laddering." Positions that have this type of solid market data provide the compensation group with a high degree of confidence when analyzing and developing the compensation program for the company.

Not all positions within the organization are benchmark positions. This simply means that not all jobs are available in published survey information. The job may be unique to the company. Positions that are not benchmarked are not used in the wage and salary planning process.

Typically, nonbenchmarked positions are slotted into a wage and salary structure once the market analysis is complete. Security managers should always ask, "Are our positions used in the benchmarking process?" If positions are not benchmarked, the manager may want to consider working with the compensation group to identify an appropriate published compensation survey to which their positions can be matched. If the information is determined to be unavailable, the manager may want to consider sponsoring a special survey. The goal of the security manager is to ensure their positions are reviewed annually, and that the wage and salary grade and structure are derived from current and valid market data.

Overview of a wage and salary grade structure

Once each benchmark position has been evaluated internally and competitive external market data has been obtained, a wage and salary grade structure can be developed. The compensation group develops the grade structure with minimum, midpoint and maximum ranges of pay. The grade midpoint (center of the range) that most closely matches the competitive practice target of the company's philosophy would be the grade in which each job is placed. It is a common practice in industry to have multiple wage and salary structures within an organization to meet the needs of internal equity and external market.

Grade structures are wage and salary ranges for a population of positions that are typically determined by internal ranking and external market data. Grade structures are designed to reflect the value of each position within the grade. Wage and salary grades typically have a minimum, midpoint and maximum dollar value.

Grade minimum: The range minimum defines the company's established lowest annual wage or salary for the position. This is the entry-level an employee can expect to be paid within the grade.

Grade midpoint: The range midpoint defines the company's established market or internal value targeted for positions within the grade. An employee paid at this level would be expected to perform as a fully competent contributor.

Grade maximum: The range maximum defines the company's established maximum pay for the position. An employee paid at this level would be fully proficient and seasoned in the position and may be ready to assume greater responsibilities.

Wage and salary grade ranges are typically designed by using compensation survey data on competitive practices. Positions are analyzed using the compensation survey's position descriptions and are matched to the company's descriptions. Factors such as position scope, job knowledge, and accountability, among other factors, are compared to the descriptions in the compensation survey. Once a good match between the company position and the survey position is made, the company uses the market data in the survey to incorporate their company's compensation philosophy. Positions with similar market targets are then placed together in a company-designed salary grade level. The midpoint of the grade that best reflects the market target is used to assign each position.

The expectation from human resources/compensation is that security managers will utilize the grade structure as a compensation tool. The placement of individuals within the grade is recognition of job proficiency. The midpoint of the range represents the market target for positions in the grade and is appropriate for employees who are fully competent and proficient in their job.

Salary grade

Typically, a salary grade range (minimum to maximum) for executive, management, and professional positions will be plus and minus 20% of the midpoint. The difference between grades is typically around 12–15% between midpoint dollars. An example of a salary grade would be:

Minimum	Midpoint	Maximum
$80,000	$100,000	$120,000

Wage grade

Generally, a wage grade range (minimum to maximum) for nonexempt positions will be plus and minus 15% of the midpoint. The difference between grades is typically around 8–12% between midpoint dollars. An example of a wage grade would be:

Minimum	Midpoint	Maximum
$42,500	$50,000	$57,500

An employee who has recently been promoted, or who is new to the position and still learning the nature and scope of the work, would be placed between the minimum and midpoint of the grade range. This could be an employee who has just started with the company and is new to the role, or a recent college graduate not yet fully competent and proficient compared to a seasoned employee.

An employee's placement within the grade structure should reflect job proficiency. If an employee is fully competent in the job, the employee's placement within the grade structure should be plus or minus five or 10% of the midpoint of the grade range. The midpoint represents the market value for the position, coupled with the internal ranking of the job within the company.

Employees paid above the midpoint or close to the maximum are usually those individuals very seasoned in the job and are ready to assume greater responsibilities in the next career level. These employees are the most seasoned for the position or are taking on additional accountabilities normally found at a higher level. If the employee is assuming more responsibility and is being paid 15% or more above the midpoint, the individual should be considering for a career move.

Broadbanding grade structure

There is another and very different type of grade structure, called "broadbanding." This type of grade structure is used by fewer companies than other structures.

Broadbanding is a pay structure that collapses multiply wage and salary grades and ranges into one large band. For example, if the previous traditional grade structure had 25 grades, the new broadband structure might have as few as seven large bands that represent the consolidation of the grades. The spread from minimum to maximum could be 150–200% and some cases more.

Each salary band will encompass a larger number of positions than a traditional grade structure, because the spread between the minimum and maximum of the band is so much greater. Employees in a banding type of structure are sometimes confused regarding their potential wage and salary opportunities, particularly at the entry level (minimum). Their internal job value appears distorted due to the wide range of diverse occupations and levels of positions in the band. However, most companies employ control points or market competitive practice for each job within the band.

Managing without a grade structure

A few major companies do not have a defined grade structure, but use only competitive practice for each position. Using compensation survey data, the company assesses the market price of as many positions as possible to gain a true market target for each job. Those jobs that did not have market data would be placed with a job of equal internal value and be given a market target. The company would then administer its pay program in a similar fashion to companies with grade structures or pay ranges.

Determining the salary compa-ratio

To measure an individual's salary as compared to the midpoint of the wage and salary range, the compensation group uses a simple formula that can also be used by each individual manager; the term is called a "compa-ratio," or the ratio of an employee's pay to the midpoint of the wage or salary grade structure. A compa-ratio is determined by dividing the employee pay by the midpoint of the grade. A compa-ratio can be applied to all employees in a grade, a department or the entire organization. The compa-ratio can also be used for comparison to survey market data. Following is an example for determining an individual's compa-ratio to the grade midpoint:

Employee	Annual Base Pay	Grade Midpoint	Compa-Ratio
John Smith	$85,000	$100,000	15.0% below midpoint
Roger Jones	$114,400	$100,000	14.4% above midpoint

In the first example above, John Smith is paid 85% of the midpoint of the range, or presumably below the company's market target for a fully competent employee. Considering John's grade placement at 15% below midpoint, we must assume the employee is either new to the job or still not meeting the full requirements of the position.

The second example indicates that Roger Jones is paid almost 15% above the midpoint of the grade. This would indicate that Roger is highly competent and proficient, and may be ready to assume additional accountabilities.

The compa-ratio formula can be used to determine the overall market or midpoint position for all the jobs in a business unit. Another use for determining the compa-ratio is gauging where the total population of the unit or organization lies as a percentage of the midpoint. In the above example, the compa-ratio for both employees combined is 99.7% of the midpoint. Determining the compa-ratio provides security managers with another snapshot of how successful they are in meeting the company's philosophy on pay practices.

Managing changes in employee job responsibilities

As a security manager, you are responsible for ensuring your employees are appropriately paid for performing their assigned job duties and for their overall job performance. As an example, consider the situation when you have asked an employee to assume more complex duties and take on significantly more responsibility in the unit. The following process will help you in this area of salary administration.

1. Prepare a Position Analysis Questionnaire describing the new job content, responsibilities, education, experience, and certification requirements. You may find it valuable to have the employee collaborate in developing the analysis questionnaire. Once completed, the document can be given to your designated compensation specialist to develop a new formal job description.
2. Internally rank the new job based solely on your perceived internal value in relationship to all other positions in the security unit's hierarchy.
3. Advise your compensation specialist of your job hierarchy placement and the justification for your decision. Request that the job content be matched to one or more current compensation surveys to obtain the base wage or salary level consistent with the company's pay philosophy, e.g. weighted average, median, 75th percentile, etc. A modest increase in job content and responsibility might support a one-level pay grade increase; a significant change in content and responsibility might warrant a two or more level pay grade change.
4. Calculate the compa-ratio by dividing the employee's current wage or salary by the grade midpoint (100% value). As an example, assume the employee's salary is $60,000 and the salary grade midpoint is $80,000; the compa-ratio will be 75%. Generally, this places the current salary below the minimum of the targeted wage and salary range. For an employee assuming new duties and responsibilities significantly greater than the previous job, the incumbent's salary should be less than the midpoint value and typically at 80–90% of the midpoint. Considering your employee's grade placement at 75% of midpoint, it indicates the employee at this time, needs to be considered for a salary adjustment to the minimum of the range or higher.
5. A wage or salary increase for the employee would normally be based on the survey market data, the employee's current performance and projected time to become fully competent in the new position. A five percent adjustment would place the employee at the salary grade minimum. This increase is normally considered a promotional adjustment, not a scheduled merit increase. A merit increase may be appropriate in addition to the five% promotional adjustment, or may be awarded at the normally scheduled performance review.
6. This is typically an appropriate time in the process to discuss the final job description content and your performance expectations in the new position with the employee. It is also the right time to inform the incumbent of the promotional salary increase, percentage amount and, if appropriate, the new salary grade.
7. Ensure the employee that you have worked closely with the compensation specialist to be fair and equitable in your actions, and that you are always available to discuss pay issues.

Planning and developing your compensation budget

Budget preparation is handled differently in each organization. Regardless of the budget process, the final figures are normally predicated on anticipated company income and profit projections. Some of the diverse approaches include the following examples.

- Some companies ask the human resources/compensation group to submit wage and salary increase percentage projections based on last year's wage and salary costs, and then apply a fixed percentage figure using published survey projections for the coming year within the same industry. In addition, funds will be established for promotions, cash bonuses and cash incentive awards for any eligible employees in the unit.
- In other companies, senior management may ask human resources/compensation to make recommendations based on where the organization's overall market position is compared to the company's target to the market using published survey information.
- Another approach companies use would be to ask the security managers to submit their wage and salary increase projections for each employee using last year's budget percentage amount for merit and promotion increases, new hire projections, cash bonuses, and incentives awards. This amount would be rolled-up into the overall company's compensation budget.
- Some companies will apply a current or projected cost of living (COLA) figure to wage and salary costs and this becomes the basis for pay increases. Often the COLA is not used exclusively, but in conjunction with compensation survey analysis for developing the merit adjustment program.

When administering the security unit's compensation budget, keep the following key considerations in mind.

- With the assistance of the compensation specialist, be sure you know how the security pay levels compare to the wage and salary survey competitive practices. Request the compa-ratio figures for your unit's population to help you determine budget requirements.
- Review the "benchmark" positions in the security unit and reevaluate the internal ranking of each job. Nonbenchmark positions should also be examined. Any needed changes of your evaluation of these jobs might affect your wage and salary budget needs.
- Identify the performance level of each employee. Determine which method to use for distributing the available wage and salary increase funds. For example, if you have 10 staff members to evaluate and reward, rank their individual performance based on a predetermined set of criteria. Employee performance will not be the same, and typically a bell-shaped curve will determine the distribution, from no increase to exceptional performance increase.

- Carefully review each employee for potential wage and salary grade movement within the unit to determine how that movement might translate into additional budget requirements. A 5% pay increase could be seen as constituting a promotion to a higher grade.
- Try to avoid any surprises for the coming budget year. For example, do you anticipate the labor market to change or become dramatically more vulnerable due to national or world events that could affect your retention of current employees and your ability to recruit new personnel? If so, this might be another basis for budget discussions with your compensation specialist.

Becoming well versed in these administrative items will assist you in developing and monitoring your pay program.

Security Job Descriptions

4

Preparing a job description

Job descriptions are important to any wage and salary program. A comprehensive job description establishes a baseline understanding of each position to be used by both human resources and management to develop programs for recruitment, training and salary administration. Typically, the security manager completes a "Position Analysis Questionnaire" to define the tasks, responsibilities, degree of supervision, level of experience, education, etc., required for a position. This exercise is the foundation for the compensation specialists to write a formal, standardized job description.

Underpinning the effort to standardize and increase pay levels of security professionals are the development and acceptance of a set of position descriptions that is widely accepted outside of the security community. It is impossible to accurately assess compensation levels based on job titles alone. Using accurate, detailed job descriptions can ensure pay rates are comparable for comparable positions, and help eliminate the huge swings in compensation levels that happen when security roles are assessed independently by various companies. Accurate job descriptions are the first step in transitioning security compensation management from an ad hoc, "thumb-in-the-air" approach to a system accepted by the human resources community and senior management.

Job descriptions encompass a multitude of variables in characterizing a given position. They include the size of the company, the geographic area served, the reporting structure, and where the position fits in the organization. Translating the characteristics of a job to an appropriate compensation level requires that the supervisor take the time to document the essential elements of the job. Otherwise, the position can be devalued, which is the number one mistake that people make. Too often, people submit a budget based on job titles, rather than on a more substantive assessment of the elements of the job. Following are some elements of a good job description.

Scope: A job description generally summarizes the scope and purpose of the position in about three sentences. Emphasis is on describing the purpose of the job, not the operational components. The best approach is to think on the "macro" level about what the position needs to accomplish, being careful not to get caught up in the details of how it is accomplished. Also, how many other employees or contractors would the incumbent supervise, either directly or indirectly?

Degree of supervision: Does the job require work guidance, immediate supervision, general supervision, or only direction? For example, if the job requires little supervision, the incumbent is responsible for developing a plan for the scope of a task and the timetable for completing it. They are responsible to the employer and manager only on the basis of results.

Impact/responsibility: To what extent do the actions taken in performing the job affect the success or failure of the department, and of the organization? It is important to consider the positive and negative consequences related to a position's span of influence.

Job descriptions should not be written to sound like a set of instructions for how to do a job. For example, instead of stating that a job entails responsibility for the physical security of a building, some job descriptions tend to get into the tiresome details of how that job is accomplished, e.g., the person is responsible for issuing parking stickers, making sure the access control system works, or whatever. That information is more appropriate for inclusion in working instructions or a training document, not a job description.

Job descriptions should also include required years of experience and education levels only as they apply to the specific job at hand. Too often, numbers like "10 years of experience" make job descriptions sound like they are trying to impress someone. Degree requirements should also be specifically related to the job. In short, nothing should be included in a job description that cannot be supported based on the work and performance requirement of the position. Requests for certifications are also often arbitrary and not related to the job. Again, job descriptions should be kept at a "macro" level, and not include too many details or unique aspects of a company.

In 2002 the Foushée Group, Inc. published the first extensive Security and Compliance Compensation Study. Information about more than 60 specific job descriptions was gathered, along with matching compensation data. This chapter contains those descriptions as they have been fine-tuned, and others added, to the present date. These job descriptions are the groundwork to help you define the profession and its elements.

The following job descriptions and data were obtained from the Security and Compliance Compensation Survey Report conducted and published by the Foushée Group, Inc. in 2013.

Top global security executive

Job Code 100

Job description

This is the most senior executive security position in the organization with direct line responsibility. This position has global accountability for developing, and directing the organization security program. Directs the domestic and international staff in identifying, developing, implementing, and maintaining security processes across the organization to reduce risks, respond to incidents, and limit exposure to liability in all areas of financial, physical, network/information technology, and personal risk. Through subordinate managers, coordinates and implements site security, operations, and activities to ensure protection of executives, managers, employees, physical and information assets, while ensuring optimal use of personnel and equipment. Develops and delivers service in response to criminal financial loss, counterfeiting, crimes against persons, sabotage, threats, emergencies, illegal acts, and property or environmental crimes. Accountable for state-of-the-art technology solutions and innovative security management techniques to safeguard the organization's assets and correct security vulnerabilities with new and legacy information technology systems. May be responsible for ensuring the safety of all network and information system environments for the corporation and operating business units. Incumbent may be responsible for network/information systems (IS) technical security architecture, network and system designs, implementation and management of systems and programs for the prevention of system hacking and virus protection. Develops and implements intrusion detection systems to prevent abuse and virus release within the organization. Develops standards and policies worldwide for compliance with government rules, regulations, laws, and treaties regarding security requirements for import and export of products. Directs the approach, deployment and execution of the most sensitive investigations. Develops relationships with high-level law enforcement and international counterparts to include in-country security and international security agencies, intelligence, and private sector counterparts worldwide.

Qualification guidelines

Master's degree or international equivalent in an area of study relevant to this position and more than 20 years experience with a major corporation and/or law enforcement, intelligence, or private sector security organization; or bachelor's degree or international equivalent in an area of study relevant to this position and more than 25 years experience with a major corporation and/or law enforcement, intelligence, public, or private sector security organization. Has demonstrated experience and exposure in the international security arena. Certification preferred.

Second level global security executive
Job Code 101

Job description
This is the most senior security management position of a major operating unit (sector, group, or large division) level. This position can have domestic and international security accountabilities for the operating unit. Directs the development and implementation of the operating unit's security policies and programs. Directs the domestic and international staff in identifying, developing, implementing, and maintaining security processes across the operating unit to reduce risks, respond to incidents, and limit exposure to liability in order to reduce financial loss to the organization. Identifies significant security risks, designs and implements strategies, and programs to prevent and reduce loss of the organization's assets. Establishes appropriate standards and risk control associated with intellectual property within the operating unit. Directs, coordinates, and implements site security, operations, and activities to ensure the protection of executives, managers, employees, physical, and information assets, while ensuring optimal use of personnel and equipment. Develops and delivers preventative programs and services to protect against criminal financial loss, counterfeiting, crime against persons, sabotage, threats, emergencies, illegal acts, and property or environmental crimes. Researches and deploys state-of-the-art technology solutions and innovative security management techniques to safeguard the operating units assets. Directs the approach, deployment, and execution of investigations, and directs team-based system development efforts. Develops and manages the capital and expense budget for the unit's worldwide security operations. Develops close relationships with high-level law enforcement and international counterparts to include in-country security and international security agencies, intelligence, and private sector counterparts worldwide. Briefs executive management on status of security issues. Develops a consensus position within an organization climate of diverse operational activities and often-conflicting regulations imposed by agencies with regulatory jurisdiction. Provides leadership direction to the management and professional staff within the organization unit.

Qualification guidelines
Master's degree or international equivalent in an area of study relevant to this position and more than 15 years experience with a major law enforcement, intelligence, public service or private sector security organization; or bachelor's degree or international equivalent in an area of study relevant to this position and more than 20 years experience with a major law enforcement, intelligence, public, or private sector security organization. Has demonstrated experience and exposure in the international security arena. Certification preferred.

Top security executive, international
Job Code 200

Job description

This is the most senior international security position in the organization with direct line responsibility. This position does not have domestic security accountabilities, but is domiciled in the United States. Accountable for developing, implementing, and directing a responsible company-wide international security program. Directs the international security staff in identifying, developing, implementing, and maintaining security processes across the organization to reduce risks, respond to incidents, and limit exposure to liability in order to reduce financial loss to the organization. Within the international operations of the organization, identifies significant security risks, designs and implements strategies and programs to prevent and reduce loss of the organization's assets. Through subordinate site managers operating in an international environment or facility, coordinates and implements site security, operations and activities to ensure protection of executives, managers, employees, physical assets, intellectual properties, and information assets, while ensuring optimal use of personnel and equipment. Develops and implements policies and programs in response to criminal financial loss, crime against persons, sabotage, threats, emergencies, illegal acts, and property or environmental crimes. May coordinate the safety of international network and information system environments for the international business units. Through subordinate site managers operating in an international environment or facility, may be responsible for network/IS technical security architecture, network and system designs, implementation and management of systems and programs for the prevention of system hacking and virus protection. Working with in-country agencies and staff, directs the approach, deployment, and execution of investigations. Maintains close relationships with high-level law enforcement, intelligence, and private sector counterparts to include in-country security and international security agencies. Researches and deploys state-of-the-art technology solutions and innovative security management techniques to safeguard the organization's assets.

Qualification guidelines

Master's degree or international equivalent in an area of study relevant to this position and more than 15 years experience with a major corporation and/or law enforcement, intelligence, public service or private sector security organization; or bachelor's degree or international equivalent in an area of study relevant to this position and more than 20 years experience with a major law enforcement, intelligence, public, or private sector security organization. Must have demonstrated experience and exposure in the international security arena. Certification preferred.

Senior regional manager, international security

Job Code 210

Job description

Plans and directs the organization's largest international geographic region(s) security function under senior management direction. Develops, implements, and manages the strategic and tactical planning for the region's security services. The senior regional manager position has the largest geographical area of accountability in terms of organization assets, facilities, number, and size of operating sites as opposed to a regional manager. Directs the international security staff in identifying, developing, implementing, and maintaining security processes across the organization to reduce risks, respond to incidents, and limit exposure to liability in order to reduce financial loss to the organization. Identifies significant security risks, designs and implements strategies and programs to prevent and reduce loss of the organization's assets. Coordinates and implements site security, operations and activities to ensure protection of executives, managers, employees, physical assets, intellectual properties, and information assets, while ensuring optimal use of personnel and equipment. Develops and implements policies, procedures, standards, training, and methods for identifying and protecting intellectual property assets, personnel, property, facilities, operations, or material from unauthorized disclosure, misuse, theft, assault, vandalism, product tampering, espionage, sabotage, or financial loss. Working with in-country agencies and staff, directs the approach, deployment, and execution of investigations, and directs team-based system development efforts. Maintains close relationships with high-level law enforcement, intelligence, and private sector counterparts to include in-country security and international security agencies. Researches and deploys state-of-the-art technology solutions and innovative security management techniques to safeguard the organization's assets. Briefs senior management on status of international security issues. Develops a consensus position within an organization's climate of diverse operational activities and often-conflicting regulations imposed by agencies and countries with regulatory jurisdiction.

Qualification guidelines

Master's degree or international equivalent in an area of study relevant to this position and more than 10 years experience with a major law enforcement, intelligence, public service or private sector security organization; or bachelor's degree or international equivalent in an area of study relevant to this position and more than 15 years experience with a major law enforcement, intelligence, public, or private sector security organization. Must have demonstrated experience and exposure in the international security arena. Certification preferred.

Regional manager, international security
Job Code 220

Job description

Plans and directs operations in an international geographical region security function under senior management direction. Develops, implements, and manages the strategic and tactical planning for the regions international security services. This position would have a smaller geographic area of accountability in terms of organization assets, facilities, number and size of sites as opposed to a senior regional manger, international security. This position would typically be domiciled in the United States. Develops, implements, and manages regional strategic planning and coordination of the security function aligned with the organization's overall objectives. Provides regional security leadership to the sites and establishes the regions security business plan. Develops, plans, organizes, and directs the activities of on-site security managers and ensures that their actions comply with legal and regulatory requirements. Develops and implements policies, procedures, standards, training, and methods for identifying and protecting information, personnel, property, facilities, operations, or material from unauthorized disclosure, misuse, theft, assault, vandalism, product tampering, espionage, sabotage, or loss. Develops and manages business critical projects and programs with significant financial and/or legal impact on a regional level. Develops and documents standards for measuring efficiency and effectiveness of security operations. Plans, develops, and implements procedures to obtain, maintain, secure, analyze, account for, and provide information from assessment reports. Manages complex security improvement programs across business units, service organizations and regional geographies. Develops regional business plans and maintains close relationships with high-level law enforcement, intelligence, and private sector counterparts to include in-country security and international security agencies. Briefs senior and executive management on status of security issues. Manages the activities and provides leadership direction to the professional, technical, and support staff within the regions of the organizational unit. May be required to speak one or more languages of the region.

Qualification guidelines

Master's degree or international equivalent in an area of study relevant to this position and more than 8 years experience with a major law enforcement, intelligence, public service or private sector security organization; or bachelor's degree or international equivalent in an area of study relevant to this position and more than 12 years experience with a major law enforcement, intelligence, public, or private sector security organization. Must have demonstrated experience and exposure in the international security arena. Certification preferred.

Manager, international investigation
Job Code 225

Job description

Plans and directs the international investigative function under senior management direction. Accountable for implementing the organization's international investigative programs and strategies. Implements the policies, procedures, and systems required to maintain and enhance the international organizational investigative mission. Interprets and applies laws, orders, rules, and regulations pertaining to international investigations. Plans and conducts investigative operations, staff investigative requirements and oversees training of subordinate investigators overseas, in the complete spectrum of investigative techniques. Directs, plans, and carries out the most sensitive and complex investigations, investigative support operations and investigative staff projects. Develops and documents standards for measuring the efficiency and effectiveness of international investigative operations. For overseas operations, evaluates and applies in-depth knowledge to establish standards of investigative efforts required, scope and depth of fact finding needed, proper use of investigative techniques, and conclusions of investigations. Plans, develops, and implements procedures to obtain, maintain, secure, analyze, file, and account for investigative reports to appropriate in-country officials. Oversees planning and conducts extremely sensitive and complex investigations, and briefs senior and executive management on the status of these investigations. Participates and handles extremely sensitive or high profile investigations that may have political or social ramifications within the public/international country domain. Directs briefings with international law enforcement, department and corporate staff, and coordinates the use of necessary resources to achieve company objectives. Interacts with all levels within the organization, and acts as duty expert on investigative techniques. Maintains expert knowledge of specific requirements imposed by foreign government agencies, consulting with other members of the security function, as well as consulting with operating unit and field personnel. Keeps management informed on major accomplishments, issues, and concerns. Trains and develops staff.

Qualification guidelines

Master's degree or international equivalent in an area of study relevant to this position and more than 6 years experience with a major law enforcement, intelligence, public service or private sector security organization; or bachelor's degree or international equivalent in an area of study relevant to this position and more than 10 years experience with a major law enforcement, intelligence, public, or private sector security organization. Must have demonstrated experience and exposure in the international security arena. Certification preferred.

Top security executive, domestic
Job Code 300

Job description

This is the most senior domestic security management position in the organization with direct line responsibility. This position is accountable for developing, implementing, and directing a responsible domestic security program for the organization. Directs the security staff in identifying, developing, implementing, and maintaining security processes across the organization to reduce risks, respond to incidents, and limit exposure to liability in order to reduce financial loss to the organization. Identify significant security risks, design, and implement strategies and programs to prevent/reduce loss of organization assets. Implement risk reduction through increased security awareness. Through subordinate managers, coordinates and implements site security, operations, and activities to ensure protection of executives, managers, employees, physical, and information assets, while ensuring optimal use of personnel and equipment. Develops and ensures services in response to criminal financial loss, crimes against persons, sabotage, threats, emergencies, illegal acts, and property or environmental crimes. May be responsible for ensuring the safety of all network and information system environments for the corporation and operating business units. Incumbent may be responsible for network/IS technical security architecture, network and system designs, implementation and management of systems and programs for the prevention of system hacking and virus protection. Develops and implements intrusion detection systems to prevent abuse and virus release within the organization. Researches and deploys state-of-the-art technology solutions and innovative security management techniques to safeguard organization assets. Directs the approach, deployment, and execution of investigations, and directs team-based system development efforts. Develops and manages the capital and expense budget for the unit's domestic security operations. Develops close relationships with high-level domestic law enforcement and international counterparts to include in-country security and international security agencies, intelligence, and private sector counterparts. Briefs senior and executive management on status of security issues. Develops consensus within an organization from operational activities and regulations imposed by agencies with regulatory jurisdiction.

Qualification guidelines

Master's degree in an area of study relevant to this position and more than 15 years experience with a major corporation and/or law enforcement, intelligence, public service or private sector security organization; or bachelor's degree or international equivalent in an area of study relevant to this position and more than 20 years experience with a major law enforcement, intelligence, public, or private sector security organization. Has had exposure in the international security arena. Certification preferred.

Senior manager, threat analysis

Job Code 303

Job description

Plans, directs, identifies, develops, and executes the organizations research and threat analysis function regarding unevaluated complex information that may have corporate sensitivity and significant organizational, economic, political, military, and national ramifications. Position requires simultaneous response to legal, political, international, operational, and organizational aspects to resolve interpretations of threats and risks. Manages the research, analysis, coordination, publishing, and briefs on security threats, nontechnical risks and geopolitical issues in diverse geographical areas in foreign countries that have the potential of affecting the organization's businesses and employees. Assesses unforeseen developments and difficulties encountered and recommends changes in direction and approach. Works with global security leadership efforts to define and advance threat and risk concerns. Develops internal and external contacts to focuses on threat and risk issues. Manages and conducts research into various reference archives and databases to extract information contributing to threat and risk analysis or due diligence and background investigation research. Develops recommendations from analyzing complex reports to analyze and predict threat and risk issues. Maintains liaison throughout appropriate company functional entities and external counterparts. Develops and presents threat and risk information to senior management, and external organizations. Manages the coordination and issues technical guidance to other functions involved in the research and collection of security and geopolitical information. Develops, trains, and directs personnel in the threat analysis function.

Qualification guidelines

Master's degree in an area of study relevant to this position and more than 10 years experience with a major law enforcement, intelligence, public, or private sector security organization; or bachelor's degree in an area of study relevant to this position and more than 15 years experience with a major law enforcement, intelligence, public, or private sector security organization. Conducts archival research and analysis, and evaluates the validity of data, analyzes information reports, and presents a coherent global security position.

Senior threat analyst IV

Job Code 306

Job description

Works under consultative direction toward predetermined goals and objectives. Assignments are usually self-initiated. Determines and pursues courses of action necessary to obtain desired results, and makes recommendations and changes in departmental policies and procedures. Work is checked through consultation and agreement, rather than formal review of the supervisor. Researches and writes in-depth reports and advisories on security risks to employees and operations world-wide. Provides rapid assessments of potentially imminent security situations, sensitive developments, and complex threat issues. Identifies, tracks, and monitors emerging security threats and trends. Keeps abreast of changing geopolitical events, which could impact stability and operations. Provides research, analysis, coordination, publishing, and briefs on security threats, nontechnical risks and geopolitical issues in diverse geographical areas in foreign countries or domestic operations that have the potential of affecting the organization's businesses and employees. Assesses unforeseen threat developments and recommends changes in security direction and approach. Prepares briefs on strategic intelligence issues for senior management. Maintains internal and external contacts that focuses on threat and risk issues. Manages and conducts research into various reference archives and databases to extract information contributing to threat and risk analysis or due diligence and background investigation research. Maintains liaison throughout appropriate company functional entities and external counterparts.

Qualification guidelines

Master's degree in an area of study relevant to this position and more than 4 years experience with a major law enforcement, intelligence, public, or private sector security organization; or bachelor's degree in an area of study relevant to this position and more than 8 years experience with a major law enforcement, intelligence, public, or private sector security organization. Knowledge reasoning to conduct archival research and analysis and evaluate the validity of data and analyze information reports.

Senior manager, protective services (headquarters)

Job Code 310

Job description

Plans, develops, and directs the organization's protective services function under senior management direction. Develops, manages, and executes protective services programs for the chairman, CEO, president, members of the board of directors and other executives of the organization and their families. Responsible for protective programs to include personal protection, corporate facilities, residence, airfield and event security, ground and air transportation, protocol, personal assistance, and special projects. Manages on- and off-site planning, coordination, and execution of plans for visiting dignitaries to include the board of directors, CEO's of other organizations, major account customers, heads of state, political leaders, and others. Directs the planning and execution of major corporate events and visits by dignitaries and VIP guests of the organization to ensure a safe environment. Develops and implements protective service objectives, plans, and procedures. Implements the policies, procedures, and systems required for maintaining and enhancing the overall organization's protective services organizational mission. Develops and documents standards of measurement of quality and effectiveness of programs. Manages all security-related issues associated with corporate aircraft facility, to including the security of the aircraft. Responsibility includes measures to protect aircraft flight facilities, in flight, and at domestic and international locations where aircraft are parked during transit status. Develops and maintains wide range of intra- and inter-agency coordination. Determines need for and manages procurement, installation, and operational instruction of security equipment required at the residence, vacation homes or offices of executives. Develops and maintains personal profiles and conducts risk assessment of all personnel covered by protective services. Identifies groups, individuals and merging technologies that may pose threat to executives. Keeps management informed on major accomplishments, issues, and concerns. Develops, trains, and directs the personnel in the protective service function.

Qualification guidelines

Master's degree or international equivalent in an area of study relevant to this position and more than 8 years experience with a major law enforcement, intelligence, public service or private sector security organization; or bachelor's degree or international equivalent in an area of study relevant to this position and more than 12 years experience with a major law enforcement, intelligence, public, or private sector security organization. Must have demonstrated experience and exposure in the international security arena. Certified protection professional (CPP) and/or certified protection officer (CPO) preferred.

Senior protective services agent IV
Job Code 314

Job description

Works under consultative direction toward predetermined goals and objectives Assignments are usually self-initiated. Determines and pursues courses of action necessary to obtain desired results, and makes recommendations and changes to departmental policies and procedures. Work is checked through consultation and agreement, rather than formal review of the supervisor. Executes protective services programs for the chairman, CEO, president, members of the board of directors, and other executives of the company and their families. Ensures the execution of off-site planning, coordination, and execution of programs for visiting dignitaries to include the board of directors, CEO's of other organizations, major account customers, heads of state, political leaders, and others. Manages the planning and execution of major corporate events and visits by dignitaries and VIP guest of the organization to ensure a safe environment. Responsible for protective programs to include personal protection, corporate facilities, residence, airfield and event security, ground and air transportation, protocol, personal assistance, and special projects. Evaluates and documents standards of measurement of quality and effectiveness of programs. Oversees measures to protect aircraft flight facilities, in flight, and at domestic and international locations where aircraft are parked during transit status. Maintains a wide range of intra- and interagency coordination. Ensures the procurement, installation, and operational instruction of security equipment required at the residence, vacation homes, or offices of executives. Participates in the development and maintenance of personal profiles and conducts risk assessment of all personnel covered by protective services. Identifies groups, individuals, and merging technologies that may pose threat to executives. Represents the organization in intra- and intercompany committees. Provides leadership to less experienced protective service agents and technicians.

Qualification guidelines

Master's degree or international equivalent in an area of study relevant to this position and more than 4 years experience with a major law enforcement, intelligence, public service or private sector security organization; or bachelor's degree or international equivalent in an area of study relevant to this position and more than 10 years experience with a major law enforcement, intelligence, public, or private sector security organization. Must have demonstrated experience and exposure in the international security arena. CPP and/or CPO preferred.

Protective services agent III

Job Code 315

Job description

Works under general direction, exercising reasonable latitude in determining protective service techniques to accomplish objectives. Work is reviewed upon completion for adequacy in meeting objectives. Participates in providing protective service programs for the chairman, CEO, president, members of the board of directors, and other executives of the organization and their families. Will participate in protective programs to include personal protection, corporate facilities, residence, airfield and event security, ground and air transportation, protocol, personal assistance, and special projects. Coordinates off-site planning, and execution of plans for visiting dignitaries to include the board of directors, CEO's of other companies, major account customers, heads of state, political leaders and others. Contributes to the planning and execution of small to medium corporate events, and visits by dignitaries and VIP guests of the organization to ensure a safe environment. Identifies security-related issues associated with corporate aircraft facility, including the security of the aircraft. Responsibility includes measures to protect aircraft at home flight facility, in flight, and at domestic and international locations where aircraft are parked during transit status. Maintains a wide range of intra- and interagency coordination. Assists in determining the need for procurement, installation, and operational instruction of security equipment required at the residence, vacation homes, or offices of executives. May contribute to maintaining personal profiles and conduct risk assessments of all personnel covered by protective services. Identifies groups, individuals, and merging technologies that may pose threat to executives. Participates in professional forums and maintains currency with trends and developments in the executive protection field. May act as a lead person or technical expert on small to medium projects.

Qualification guidelines

Bachelor's degree or international equivalent in an area of study relevant to this position and more than 8 years experience with a major law enforcement, intelligence, public, or private sector security organization. Must have demonstrated experience and exposure in the international security arena. Must meet any physical requirements for defensive combat protective personnel. Also must qualify with weapons. Must be able to perform duties wearing personal protective equipment. CPP and/or CPO preferred.

Protective services agent II

Job Code 316

Job description

Works under general supervision. Follows established procedures. Work is reviewed systematically through completion for adequacy in meeting objectives. With guidance, provides protective services for executives of the organization and their families as directed. Contributes to and participates in the protective programs to include personal protection, corporate facilities, residence, airfield and event security, ground and air transportation, protocol, personal assistance, and special projects. Assists with on- and off-site planning, coordination, and execution of plans for visiting dignitaries to include the board of directors, CEO's of other organization's, major account customers, heads of state, political leaders, and others. Assists with the planning and execution of small to medium corporate events, and visits by dignitaries and VIP guests of the corporation to ensure a safe environment. Assists in providing security-related issues associated with corporate aircraft facility, including the security of the aircraft. Responsibility includes carrying out predetermined measures to protect aircraft at home flight facility, in flight, and at domestic and international locations where aircraft are parked during transit status. Provides necessary assistance in maintaining a wide range of intra- and interagency coordination. Assists in determining the needs for procurement, installation, and operational instruction of security equipment required at the residence, vacation homes, or offices of executives. With guidance from senior staff, develops and maintains personal profiles and conducts risk assessment of all personnel covered by protective services. Identifies groups, individuals, and merging technologies that may pose threat to executives. Participates in professional forums and maintains currency with trends and developments in the executive protection field. May act as a lead person or technical advisor on small projects.

Qualification guidelines

Bachelor's degree or international equivalent in an area of study relevant to this position and more than 6 years experience with a major law enforcement, intelligence, public, or private sector security organization. Must have demonstrated experience and exposure in the international security arena. Must meet any physical requirements for defensive combat protective personnel. Also must qualify with weapons. Must be able to perform duties wearing personal protective equipment. CPP and/or CPO preferred.

Protective services agent I

Job Code 317

Job description

Works under close supervision. Performs tasks from detailed instructions and established procedures. Work is reviewed for soundness of technical judgment and for following the defined policies and procedures. Under direction of senior staff, provides protective services for executives of the organization and their families. Responsible for protective programs to include personal protection, corporate facilities, residence, airfield and event security, ground and air transportation, protocol, personal assistance, and special projects. Assists senior staff with on- and off-site planning, coordination, and execution of plans for visiting dignitaries. Assists senior staff with the planning and execution of small to medium corporate events, and visits by dignitaries and VIP guests of the corporation to ensure a safe environment. Responsibility includes ensuring predetermined measures met to protect aircraft at home flight facilities, in flight, and at domestic and international locations where aircraft are parked during transit status. Under direction of senior staff, works to determine the needs for procurement, installation, and operational instruction of security equipment required at the residence, vacation homes, or offices of executives. With guidance from senior staff, develops and maintains personal profiles and conducts risk assessment of all personnel covered by protective services. Identifies groups, individuals, and merging technologies that may pose threat to executives. Participates in professional forums and maintains currency with trends and developments in the executive protection field.

Qualification guidelines

Bachelor's degree or international equivalent in an area of study relevant to this position and more than 4 years experience with a major law enforcement, intelligence, public, or private sector security organization. Must meet any physical requirements for defensive combat protective personnel. Also must qualify with weapons. Must be able to perform duties wearing personal protective equipment. Certification preferred.

Director, computer, network and information security
Job Code 319

Job description

Plans, directs, and manages the computer, network and information security function within the organization to ensure its effective operation based on predetermined goals and objectives under executive management direction. Accountable for the business strategies associated with the technology needed in the security function within the organization. Develops and implements the policies, procedures, and systems required for maintaining and enhancing the overall security goals. Responsible for the research, design, development, and implementation of the organization's security and protection technologies for computer systems and applications. Responsible for the development of security plans, designs, best practices, and guidelines for existing or new technologies within network security and firewall protection. Researches, develops, maintains, and audits the analytical and technical aspects of major information and intellectual capital security systems and subsystems. Responsible for maintaining and upgrading the security integrity of computer workstations, servers, local area networks, application systems, and software. Develops security solutions for the company's virtual private networks, key public infrastructures, authentication, and directory services. Accountable for selecting, testing, installing and operation of cryptographic equipment, secure transmission of classified information, sensitive unclassified information, and protection of cryptographic principles and methods. Accountable for and directs complex surveillance of computer/network protection measures, and creates measurement tools for system vulnerability assessments. Researches, develops, contacts, and selects vendors to develop technical solutions for site security needs and presents recommendations to executive management. Briefs executive management on major accomplishments, issues, and concerns. Responsible for the selecting and developing of key security personnel for the computer, network, and information function of the organization.

Qualification guidelines

PhD in computer science and more than 7 years experience; master's degree and more than 10 years; or bachelor's degree and more than 15 years experience or other studies relevant to this position and/or in a major corporation and/or law enforcement, intelligence, public service, or private sector security organization. Has exposure in the international security arena. Certified information systems security professional (CISSP) preferred.

Manager, computer and information security

Job Code 320

Job description

Plans, develops, and directs the computer and information security function under senior management direction. Responsible for the business strategies associated with the computer and information security function within the organization. Accountable for overall planning, directing, and organizing activities of the computer and information security function, and ensure its effective operation. Implements the policies, procedures, and systems required for maintaining and enhancing the overall computer and information security organizational mission. Responsible for the research, design, development, and implementation of computer security/protection technologies for the organization's information and process systems/applications. Accountable for the computer security for classified information security and communications security. Researches, contacts, and selects vendors to develop technical solutions for site computer security needs, and presents recommendations to senior management. Develops, maintains, and audits the analytical and technical aspects of major computer security subsystems. Maintains the integrity of computer workstations, servers, local area networks, upgrading systems and software for the company. Responsible for selecting, testing, and the secure installation and operation of cryptographic equipment, secure transmission of classified information and sensitive unclassified information, and protection of cryptographic principles and methods. Responsible for identifying and mitigating threats and vulnerabilities associated with compromising electromagnetic emanations from equipment used to process classified information. Develops and provides technical support, training, and timely computer system data recovery to end-users. Directs the investigation of computer security incidents, and develops facility protection plans. Directs complex surveillance of computer protection measures, and creates measurement tools for system vulnerability assessments. Keeps senior management informed on major accomplishments, issues, and concerns. Develops, trains, and directs computer and information security personnel within the organization.

Qualification guidelines

Master's degree in computer science or other studies relevant to this position and more than 6 years experience in a major corporation and/or law enforcement, intelligence, public service, or private sector security organization; or bachelor's degree in computer science or other studies relevant to this position and more than 10 years experience with a major law enforcement, intelligence, public, or private sector security organization. Has had some exposure in the international security arena. CISSP preferred.

Senior computer and information security specialist IV
Job Code 321

Job description

Works under consultative direction toward predetermined goals and objectives. Assignments are usually self-initiated. Determines and pursues courses of action necessary to obtain desired results, and makes recommendations and changes to departmental policies and procedures. Work is checked through consultation and agreement, rather than formal review of the supervisor. Responsible for the research, design, development, and implementation of computer security/protection technologies for company information and process systems/applications. Also is accountable for the computer security for classified information security and communications security. Acts as a lead contact with vendors to develop technical solutions for site computer security needs, and makes recommendations to senior management. Develops, maintains, and audits the analytical and technical aspects of major computer security subsystems. Maintains integrity of computer workstations, servers, and local area networks by maintaining user accounts and upgrading systems and software as required. Responsible for secure installation and operation of cryptographic equipment, secure transmission of classified information and sensitive unclassified information, and protection of cryptographic principles and methods. Identifies and mitigates threats and vulnerabilities associated with compromising electromagnetic emanations from equipment used to process classified information. Provides technical support, training, and timely computer system data recovery to end-users. Oversees the investigation of computer security incidents, and acts as a lead analyst of computer facility protection plans. Conducts complex surveillance of computer protection measures, and creates measurement tools for system vulnerability assessments. Serves on internal committees to represent computer security interests. Provides oversight to the client group on appropriate procedures for computer/system security. Provides leadership to less experienced computer and information security specialists and technicians.

Qualification guidelines

Master's degree in computer science or other studies relevant to this position and more than 4 years experience in a major corporation an/or law enforcement, intelligence, public service, or private sector security organization; or bachelor's degree in computer science or other studies relevant to this position and more than 8 years experience with a major law enforcement, intelligence, public, or private sector security organization. Exposure in the international security arena is desirable. CISSP preferred.

Computer and information security specialist III

Job Code 322

Job description

Works under very limited direction. Exercises reasonable latitude in determining computer and information security techniques to accomplish objectives. Work is reviewed upon completion for adequacy in meeting objectives. Conducts research, designs, develops, and implements computer security/protection technologies for the organization's information and process systems/applications. Researches and implements computer security for classified information security and communications security. Works with vendors to develop technical solutions for site security needs. Conducts maintenance and subsequent audits of the analytical and technical aspects of major computer security subsystems within established guidelines. Maintains integrity of computer workstations, servers, and local area networks by maintaining user accounts and recommending upgrades to systems and software required. Assists in the secure installation and operation of cryptographic equipment, secure transmission of classified information and sensitive unclassified information, and protection of cryptographic principles and methodologies. Works to identify and mitigate threats and vulnerabilities associated with compromising electromagnetic emanations from equipment used to process classified information. Provides technical support, training, and timely computer system data recovery to end-users. Investigates computer security incidents, and recommends corrective actions. Conducts surveillance of computer protection measures, and creates measurement tools for system vulnerability assessments. Provides oversight to the client group on appropriate procedures for computer/system security. Provides leadership to less experienced computer and information security specialists and technicians. May act as a lead person or technical expert on medium to large projects.

Qualification guidelines

Master's degree in computer science or other studies relevant to this position and more than 3 years experience with a major corporation and/or law enforcement, intelligence, public service, or private sector security organization; or bachelor's degree in computer science or other studies relevant to this position and more than 6 years experience with a major law enforcement, intelligence, public, or private sector security organization. Some exposure in the international security arena is desirable. CISSP preferred.

Computer and information security specialist II
Job Code 323

Job description

Works is performed under general supervision. Follows established procedures. Work is reviewed systematically through completion for adequacy in meeting objectives. With guidance, conducts research, design, development, and implementation of computer security and protection technologies for organization's information and process systems/applications. Assists in the research and implementation of computer security for classified information security and communications security. Works with vendors to develop technical solutions for site security needs. Maintains integrity of computer workstations, servers, and local area networks by maintaining user accounts and recommending upgrades to systems and software required. Responds to client requests, and prepares security plans and reports based on client needs. Supports the secure installation and operation of cryptographic equipment, secure transmission of classified information and sensitive unclassified information, and protection of cryptographic principles and methodologies. Provides technical support to system users to include hardware configuration, installation, diagnostics, testing, problem resolution, system maintenance, and data recovery. Assists in the investigation of computer security incidents, and may recommend corrective actions. Acts as an alternate team lead on small computer security incidents. Conducts technical evaluations of hardware, software, and installed systems and networks. Conducts certification testing of installed systems to ensure protection strategies are properly implemented.

Qualification guidelines

Bachelor's degree in computer science or other studies relevant to this position and more than 4 years experience with a law enforcement, intelligence, public, or private sector security organization. CISSP preferred.

Computer and information security specialist I

Job Code 324

Job description

Works under close supervision. Performs tasks from detailed instructions and established procedures. Work is reviewed for soundness of technical judgment and for following the defined policies and procedures. Under direction of senior staff, evaluates, designs, and develops computer security/protection technologies for company information and process systems/applications. May assist in the implementation of computer security for classified information security and communications security. Maintains integrity of computer workstations, servers, and local area networks by maintaining user accounts and recommending upgrades to systems and software required. Responds to client requests, documenting and reporting any security incidents. Provides technical support to system users to include hardware configuration, installation, diagnostics, testing, maintenance, and data recovery. Investigates routine computer incidents under direction of a senior specialist. Assists in conducting technical evaluations of hardware, software, and installed systems and networks. Conducts routine certification testing of installed systems to ensure protection strategies are properly implemented.

Qualification guidelines

Bachelor's degree in computer science or other studies relevant to this position and a minimum of 2 years of experience with a law enforcement, intelligence, public, or private sector security organization.

Manager, network security
Job Code 325

Job description

Plans, develops, and directs the computer network security function under senior management direction. Responsible for the business strategies associated with the computer network security function within the organization. Accountable for overall planning, directing, and organizing activities of the computer network security function, and ensure its effective operation. Implements the policies, procedures, and systems required for maintaining and enhancing the overall computer network security organizational mission. Accountable for the research, design, development, and implementation of extremely complex computer network security/protection technologies for company information and network systems/applications. Accountable for the development of security plans, designs, best practices, and guidelines for existing or new technologies within network security and firewall protection. Develops virus protection security procedures to insure that e-mail and e-mail attachments are appropriately scanned and all network-attachment resources are implemented with the appropriate and updated software to prevent a computer virus infection. Develops security solutions for the company's networks and virtual private networks, key public infrastructures, authentication and directory services, ensuring the security of unauthorized access. Works closely with the business unit's information systems teams to ensure that the security baseline is complied to, in order to mitigate virus risks to the enterprise. Ensures the company's strategic platforms are compliant to security policy by performing periodic scans against policy settings. Accountable for performing periodic scans of networks to identify security vulnerabilities and provides remediation alternatives. Oversees the application and administration of security policy on network-attached resources. Develops security solutions that require resolution of extremely complex operational and integration issues to successfully deploy secure technologies. Works with vendors, external organizations, or customers to define security requirements and identify project opportunities.

Qualification guidelines

Master's degree in computer science or other studies relevant to this position and more than 6 years experience with a major corporation and/or law enforcement, intelligence, public service, or private sector security organization; or bachelor's degree in computer science or other studies relevant to this position and more than 10 years experience with a major law enforcement, intelligence, public, or private sector security organization. Some exposure in the international security arena is desirable. CISSP preferred.

Senior network security specialist IV

Job Code 326

Job description

Works under consultative direction toward predetermined goals and objectives. Assignments are usually self-initiated. Determines and pursues courses of action necessary to obtain desired results, and makes recommendations and changes to departmental policies and procedures. Work is checked through consultation and agreement, rather than formal review of the supervisor. Responsible for the research, design, development, and implementation of extremely complex computer network security/protection technologies for company information and network systems/ applications. Develops security plans, designs, best practices, and guidelines for existing or new technologies within network security and firewall protection. Develops virus protection security procedures to insure that e-mail and e-mail attachments are appropriately scanned and all network-attachment resources are implemented with the appropriate and updated software to prevent a computer virus infection. Provide security solutions for the company's networks and virtual private networks, key public infrastructures, authentication and directory services, ensuring the security of unauthorized access. Performs periodic scans of networks to identify security vulnerabilities and provide remediation alternatives. Conduct security risk assessment to ensure compliance with corporate security policies and adherence to best practices. Develops security design plans to implement, test, and manage new or existing network security technologies and strategies. Provides security solutions that require resolution of complex operational and integration issues to successfully deploy secure technologies. Serves on internal committees to represent and support computer/internet security interests. Works with vendors, external organizations, or customers to define security requirements and identify project opportunities. Provides leadership to less experienced computer and information security specialists and technicians. May act as a lead person or technical expert on large projects.

Qualification guidelines

Master's degree in computer science or other studies relevant to this position and more than 4 years experience with a major corporation and/or law enforcement, intelligence, public service or private sector security organization; or bachelor's degree in computer science or other studies relevant to this position and more than 8 years experience with a major corporation and/or law enforcement, intelligence, public, or private sector security organization. Exposure in the international security arena is desirable. CISSP preferred.

Network security specialist III

Job Code 327

Job description

Works under very limited direction. Exercises reasonable latitude in determining computer and information security techniques to accomplish objectives. Work is reviewed upon completion for adequacy in meeting objectives. Researches, designs, develops, and implements computer network security/protection technologies for the organization's information and network systems/applications. Develops, implements, and maintains extremely complex network and firewall security plans and configurations based on security requirements, project schedules, network topologies, applications, and security standards. May develop security solutions for company networks, virtual private networks and public key infrastructure, authentication, and directory services, ensuring security vulnerabilities and provides remediation alternatives. Conducts security assessments and vulnerability analysis studies of existing network to verify policies are maintained. Works with senior specialists to apply and administer virus protection security to insure that e-mail and e-mail attachments are appropriately scanned and all network-attachment resources are implemented with appropriate and updated software to prevent computer virus infection. Assist in the development and planning to detect and assess threats as well as acquire and distribute virus protection software. Provides forecasts of all work order activity including trouble ticket quantities and workload estimates to security fix agencies, vendors, and downstream organizations. Provides oversight to the client group on appropriate procedures for network computer/system security. Performs periodic scans of networks to identify security vulnerabilities and provides remediation alternatives. Provides leadership to less experienced computer and information security specialists and technicians. May act as a lead person or technical expert on medium to large projects.

Qualification guidelines

Master's degree in computer science or other studies relevant to this position and more than 3 years experience with a major corporation and/or law enforcement, intelligence, public service or private sector security organization; or bachelor's degree in computer science or other studies relevant to this position and more than 6 years experience with a major corporation and/or law enforcement, intelligence, public, or private sector security organization. Some exposure in the international security arena is desirable. CISSP preferred.

Network security specialist II

Job Code 328

Job description

Work is performed under general supervision. Follows established procedures. Work is reviewed systematically through completion for adequacy in meeting objectives. With guidance, conducts research, design, development, and implementation of computer network security and protection technologies for organization's information and network systems/applications. Develops, implements, and maintains complex network and firewall security plans and configurations based on security requirements, project schedules, network topologies, applications, and security standards. May develop security solutions for company networks, virtual private networks and public key infrastructure, authentication, and directory services, ensuring security vulnerabilities and provide remediation alternatives. Assists senior specialists in developing security standards and best practices. Works with senior specialists to administer virus protection security to insure that e-mail and e-mail attachments are appropriately scanned and all network-attachment resources are implemented with appropriate and updated software to prevent computer virus infection. Assists in the development and planning to detect and assess threats as well as acquire and distribute virus protection software. Provides forecasts of all work order activity including trouble ticket quantities and workload estimates to downstream organizations. Performs periodic scans of networks to identify security vulnerabilities and provides remediation alternatives. Review network security assessment and vulnerability analysis information to incorporate changes in common practices. Assist in security site surveys. Works to ensure that all e-mail and e-mail attachments are appropriately scanned and all network-attached resources are implemented with appropriate and updated software within assigned support group, to prevent computer virus infection. Acts as an alternate team lead on small computer security incidents. Conducts technical evaluations of hardware, software, and installed systems and networks. Conducts certification testing of installed systems to ensure that the protection strategies are properly implemented.

Qualification guidelines

Bachelor's degree in computer science or other studies relevant to this position and more than 4 years experience in corporate security and/or law enforcement, intelligence, public, or private sector security organization. CISSP preferred.

Network security specialist I

Job Code 329

Job description

Works under close supervision. Performs tasks from detailed instructions and established procedures. Work is reviewed for soundness of technical judgment and for following the defined policies and procedures. Under direction of senior staff, evaluates, designs, and develops computer network security/protection technologies for company information and network systems/applications. May assist in the implementation, development, and maintenance of moderately complex network and firewall security plans and configurations based on security requirements, project schedules, network topologies, devises, applications, and security standards. Assists senior specialists to develop security solutions for company networks, virtual private networks and public key infrastructure, authentication, and directory services, ensuring security vulnerabilities and provides remediation alternatives. Evaluates network security reports and studies to assist in the identification and resolution of potential security vulnerabilities and suspicious activities. Adheres to current security engineering practices, best practices, and standards. Assists in the administration of virus protection security to insure that e-mail and e-mail attachments are appropriately scanned and all network-attachment resources are implemented with appropriate and updated software to prevent computer virus protection. Performs periodic scans of networks to identify security vulnerabilities and recommends remediation alternatives. Assists in security site surveys. Works to ensure that all e-mail and e-mail attachments are appropriately scanned and all network-attached resources are implemented with appropriate and updated software within assigned support group, to prevent computer virus infection. Conducts routine testing of installed systems to ensure protection strategies are properly implemented.

Qualification guidelines

Bachelor's degree in computer science or other studies relevant to this position and a minimum of 2 years of experience in corporate security and/or law enforcement, intelligence, public, or private sector security organization.

Manager, domestic investigation
Job Code 330

Job description

Plans and directs the investigative function under senior management guidance. Accountable for planning, developing, and implementing the organization's investigative programs and strategies. Responsible for overall planning, organizing, and directing all actions of the investigative section of corporate security, and ensure its effective operation. Interprets all relevant data and applies appropriate laws, orders, rules, and regulations pertaining to investigations. Plans and conducts investigative operations, staff investigative requirements and oversees training of subordinate investigators in the complete spectrum of investigative techniques. Directs, plans, and carries out the most sensitive and complex investigations, investigative support operations, and investigative staff projects. Develops and documents standards for measuring the efficiency and effectiveness of investigative operations. Evaluates and applies in-depth knowledge to establish standards of investigative efforts required, scope, and depth of fact finding needed, proper use of investigative techniques, and conclusions of investigations. Plans, develops, and implements procedures to obtain, maintain, secure, analyze, file, and account for investigative reports to appropriate officials. Participates and handles extremely sensitive or high-profile investigations that may have political or social ramifications within the public domain. Oversees all investigations concerning intellectual properties to ensure that management has all necessary information for making decision to protect the organization. Directs briefings with law enforcement, department and corporate staff, and coordinates the use of necessary resources to achieve company objectives. Interacts with all levels within the organization, and acts as duty expert on investigative techniques. Maintains expert knowledge of specific requirements imposed by government agencies. Develops, trains, and directs investigative security personnel within the organization.

Qualification guidelines

Master's degree in an area of study relevant to this position and more than 5 years experience with a major law enforcement, intelligence, public service or private sector security organization; or bachelor's degree in an area of study relevant to this position and more than 8 years experience with a major law enforcement, intelligence, public, or private sector security organization. Has had some exposure in the international security arena. Certified fraud examiner (CFE) preferred.

Supervisor, domestic investigation
Job Code 331

Job description

Supervises personnel engaged in conducting security investigations to ensure compliance with the organization's policies and procedures. Works under consultative direction toward predetermined goals and objectives. Plans, organizes, and coordinates the investigative team for investigations of alleged or suspected violations of laws and regulations concerning criminal matters, associated with fraud, computer crimes, intellectual property, and other security issues. Develops investigative strategy, interviews personnel and vendors, interrogates suspects for admissions, and documents investigations with evidence so criminal and/or civil procedures are facilitated. Participates in the investigation of suspected complex and sophisticated criminal activities, which may have significant impact on health, safety, fiscal, ethical, and operations integrity. Supervises large-scale surveillance operations by determining appropriate places, persons, or activities to be observed, as well as, the time required and assets needed. Working with the investigative team establishes links between suspects and other violators by piecing together evidence uncovered from a variety of sources. Analyzes and evaluates investigative progress to reassess priorities, leads, and direction. Maintains a liaison with the organization's law department and local, state, and federal law enforcement agencies in order to achieve maximum results that support business efforts. Coordinates joint task forces, to include federal, state, and local law enforcement agencies as needed. Renders expert testimony before grand juries, courts, and administrative hearings. Prepares clear, comprehensive, and cohesive investigative reports based on established procedures. Provides development and guidance to less experienced investigators.

Qualification guidelines

Master's degree in an area of study relevant to this position and more than 4 years experience with a major law enforcement, intelligence, public service or private sector security organization; or bachelor's degree in an area of study relevant to this position and more than 8 years experience with a major law enforcement, intelligence, public, or private sector security organization. CFE preferred.

Senior investigator IV

Job Code 334

Job description

Works under consultative direction toward predetermined goals and objectives. Assignments are usually self-initiated. Determines and pursues courses of action necessary to obtain desired results, and makes recommendations and changes to departmental policies and procedures. Work is checked through consultation and agreement, rather than formal review of the supervisor. Plans, organizes, and conducts extremely difficult investigations of alleged or suspected violations of laws and regulations concerning criminal and general investigations, fraud, computer crimes and provides technical investigative services. Develops investigative strategy, interviews personnel and vendors, interrogates suspects for admissions, and documents investigations with evidence so criminal and/or civil procedures are facilitated. Maintains a liaison with the organization's law department and local, state, and federal law enforcement agencies in order to achieve maximum results that support business efforts. Investigates suspected highly complex sophisticated criminal activities, which have significant impact on health, safety, operational mission, or fiscal/ethical integrity. Conducts extremely sensitive investigations that require significant understanding of the depth and scope of potential impact that the results may have on the organization. Establishes links between suspects and other violators by piecing together evidence uncovered from a variety of sources. Analyzes and evaluates investigative progress to reassess priorities, leads, and direction. Proceeds with separate investigations that lead through immediate to principle violators. Leads large-scale surveillance operations. Determines places, persons, or activities to be observed, time required and assets needed. Coordinates joint task forces, to include federal, state, and local law enforcement agencies as well as foreign agencies as needed. Renders expert testimony before grand juries, courts, and administrative hearings. Prepares clear, comprehensive, and cohesive investigative reports based on established procedures. Oversees work and provides guidance to less experienced investigators.

Qualification guidelines

Master's degree in an area of study relevant to this position and more than 4 years experience with a major law enforcement, intelligence, public service or private sector security organization; or bachelor's degree in an area of study relevant to this position and more than 8 years experience with a major law enforcement, intelligence, public, or private sector security organization. Must have proven interview and interrogation skills. Has had some exposure in the international security arena. CFE preferred.

Investigator III
Job Code 335

Job description

Works under general direction. Exercises reasonable latitude in determining investigative techniques to accomplish objectives. Work is reviewed upon completion for adequacy in meeting objectives. The investigative caseload is assigned by management. Plans, organizes, and conducts difficult and complex investigations of alleged suspected violations of laws and regulations concerning criminal and general investigations, fraud, and computer crimes and provides technical investigative services. Develops investigative strategy, interviews personnel and vendors, interrogates suspects for admissions, and documents investigations with evidence so that criminal and/or civil procedures are facilitated. Maintains a liaison with the organization's law department and local, state, and federal law enforcement agencies in order to achieve maximum results and support business efforts. Plans and conducts investigations, investigates suspected criminal activities which have significant impact on health, safety, operational mission, or fiscal/ethical integrity. Establishes links between suspects and other violators by piecing together evidence uncovered from a variety of sources. Analyzes and evaluates investigative progress to reassess priorities, leads, and direction. Plans and directs surveillance as needed to determine places, persons or activities to be observed, time required, and number of investigators needed. Recruits and utilizes informants. Plans and times surveillance, involving the use of local law enforcement agencies. Participates in joint task forces, coordinates investigative activity with other federal, state, and local law enforcement agencies as needed to resolve jurisdictional problems in accordance with established policies. Testifies before grand juries, courts, and administrative hearings on investigation results. Prepares clear, comprehensive, and cohesive investigative reports and statistical data in a timely manner. Evaluates the latest products and techniques in communications and other technical equipment utilized in investigations, and provides advice and consultations in their use. Organizes and maintains a library of locally developed and commercial software to support investigation programs. May act as a point of contact for outside vendors. Provides guidance regarding the obtaining and handling of circumstantial, cold, and/or fragmented evidence. Based on case results, recommends corrective action aligned with operational goals and objectives.

Qualification guidelines

Bachelor's degree in an area of study relevant to this position and more than 6 years experience with a major law enforcement, intelligence, public, or private sector security organization. Must have proven interview and interrogation skills. Has had some exposure in the international security arena. CFE preferred.

Investigator II

Job Code 336

Job description

Works under general supervision. Follows established procedures. Work is reviewed systematically through completion for adequacy in meeting objectives. The investigative caseload is assigned by management or senior investigators. Conducts investigations of alleged or suspected violations and regulations concerning criminal and general investigations, fraud, and computer crimes. Works independently in planning and conducting work, but is provided assistance and guidance on assignments that involve unfamiliar issues or unusual investigative techniques. Maintains a liaison with the organization's law department and local, state, and federal law enforcement agencies in order to achieve maximum results that support business efforts. Conducts investigations, resolves conflicts based on facts, testimony, and evidence. Establishes links between suspect and other violators by linking evidence uncovered from different sources. Analyzes and evaluates investigative progress to reassess priorities, leads, and direction based on predetermined goals and objectives. Participates in and conducts surveillance, participates in joint task forces and coordinates investigative activity with other federal, state, and local law enforcement agencies as needed to exchange information or cooperate with other investigations. Testifies before grand juries, courts, and administrative hearings on investigative results. In accordance with established procedures, prepares clear, comprehensive, and cohesive investigative reports and statistical data in a timely manner. Is a participant in the identification of resource requirements to support investigations. Participates in the development of handbooks and related material covering a variety of communication systems and technical investigative programs. Helps select the latest products and assists the evaluation of proposed techniques in communications and other technical equipment. Provides advice on use of various investigative techniques. May advise and consult regarding technical aspects of an investigation to include the use of investigative devices and procedures. Recommends innovative ways to accomplish operations and investigations.

Qualification guidelines

Bachelor's degree in an area of study relevant to this position and more than 4 years experience with a major law enforcement, intelligence, public, or private sector security organization. Proven interview and interrogation skills preferred. Has had some exposure in the international security arena. CFE preferred.

Investigator I

Job Code 337

Job description

Works under close supervision. The investigative caseload is assigned by management or senior investigators. Performs tasks from detailed instructions and established procedures. Work is reviewed for soundness of investigative techniques and for following the defined policies and procedures. Management assigns caseload. Assists higher-level investigators as they plan, organize, and conduct difficult and complex investigations of alleged or suspected violations of laws or regulations concerning criminal and/or civil investigations, fraud, proprietary properties, and computer crimes and provide technical investigative services. Works with senior investigators in performing specific segments of the assignment such as gathering data, conducting interviews, searching records, securing signed documents performing surveillance, and preparing reports. Under direct supervision, performs difficult work involving the identification of issues, problems, or conditions in an ongoing investigation that requires alternative solutions. Supports senior investigators in defined investigations where work and methods are evaluated as to technical soundness, appropriateness, and effectiveness in meeting operations goals and objectives.

Qualification guidelines

Bachelor's degree in an area of study relevant to this position and more than 2 years experience with a major law enforcement, intelligence, public, or private sector security organization. Some exposure in the international security arena preferred.

Senior regional manager, domestic security

Job Code 340

Job description

Plans and directs the organization's largest geographic region(s) security function under senior management direction. Develops, implements, and manages the strategic and tactical planning for the regions security services. The senior regional manager position has the largest geographical area of accountability in terms of organization assets, facilities, number, and size of operating sites as opposed to a regional manager. Develops, implements, and manages regional strategic planning and coordination of the security function aligned with the organization's overall business objectives. Provides regional security leadership to the sites and establishes the regions security business plan. Develops, plans, organizes, and directs the activities of on-site security managers and ensures their actions comply with legal and regulatory requirements, and meet corporate and customer needs. Develops and implements policies, procedures, standards, training, and methods for identifying and protecting intellectual property assets, personnel, property, facilities, operations, or material from unauthorized disclosure, misuse, theft, assault, vandalism, product tampering, espionage, sabotage, or loss. Develop and manage business critical projects and programs with significant financial and/or legal impact on a regional level. For the region, develops, and documents standards for measuring efficiency and effectiveness of security operations. Plans, develops, and implements procedures to obtain, maintain, secure, analyze, account for, and provide information from assessment reports. Manages complex security improvement programs across business units, service organizations, and regional geographies. Develops regional business plans and maintains close relationships with high-level law enforcement, intelligence, and private sector counterparts. Briefs senior and executive management on status of security issues. Serves on senior level intra- and intercorporate committees and working groups. Manages the activities and provides leadership direction to the professional, technical, and support staff within the organization unit.

Qualification guidelines

Master's degree in an area of study relevant to this position and more than 10 years experience with a major law enforcement, intelligence, public service or private sector security organization; or bachelor's degree or international equivalent in an area of study relevant to this position and more than 15 years experience with a major law enforcement, intelligence, public, or private sector security organization. Has had exposure in the international security arena. Certification preferred.

Regional manager, domestic security

Job Code 341

Job description

Plans and directs a geographic region(s) security function under senior management direction. The manager position has the smaller geographical area of accountability in terms of organization assets, facilities, number, and size of operating sites as opposed to a senior regional manager. Develops, implements, and manages the strategic and tactical planning for the region(s) security services. Develops, implements, and manages regional strategic planning and coordination of the security function aligned with the organization's overall business objectives. Provides regional security leadership to the sites and establishes the regions security business plan. Develops, plans, organizes, and directs the activities of on-site security managers and ensures their actions comply with legal and regulatory requirements, and meet corporate and customer needs. Develops and implements policies, procedures, standards, training, and methods for identifying and protecting intellectual property assets, personnel, property, facilities, operations, or material from unauthorized disclosure, misuse, theft, assault, vandalism, product tampering, espionage, sabotage, or loss. Develops and manages business critical projects and programs with significant financial and/or legal impact on a regional level. For the region, develops and documents standards for measuring efficiency and effectiveness of security operations. Plans, develops, and implements procedures to obtain, maintain, secure, analyze, account for, and provide information from assessment reports. Manages complex security improvement programs across business units, service organizations, and regional geographies. Develops regional business plans and maintains close relationships with high-level law enforcement, intelligence, and private sector counterparts. Briefs senior and executive management on status of security issues. Serves on senior level intra- and intercorporate committees and working groups. Manages the activities and provides leadership direction to the professional, technical, and support staff within the organization unit.

Qualification guidelines

Master's degree in an area of study relevant to this position and more than 8 years experience with a major law enforcement, intelligence, public service or private sector security organization; or bachelor's degree or international equivalent in an area of study relevant to this position and more than 12 years experience with a major law enforcement, intelligence, public, or private sector security organization. Has had exposure in the international security arena. Certification preferred.

Manager, business unit security
Job Code 342

Job description

Plans and directs the business unit security function under senior management direction. Accountable for ensuring that the security programs and strategies of the organization are effectively implemented and maintained. Manages the security operations, overall planning, directing, and organizing programs of one or more major sites/facilities within a geographic region. Implements the policies, procedures, and systems required for maintaining and enhancing the overall organization's security mission. Plans, organizes, and directs the activities of business unit security managers and ensures their actions comply with legal, regulatory requirements, and customer needs. Plans and manages the most sensitive and complex security functions and develops, coordinates, and finalizes security and technical support efforts. Develops and implements policies, procedures, standards, training, and methods for identifying and protecting information, personnel, property, facilities, operations, or material from unauthorized disclosure, misuse, theft, assault, vandalism, product tampering, espionage, sabotage, or loss. Through consultation with business unit security managers establishes long and short-term security operations objectives for the organization. Plans, develops, and implements procedures to obtain, maintain, secure, analyze, account for, and provide information from assessment reports. Directs the initiation of proactive facility assessments and surveys. Based on results of trends and survey results, recommends corrective measures. Plans, acquires, and administers resources for the function, to include funding, equipment, and other resources. Develops and documents standards for measuring the efficiency and effectiveness of business unit security operations. Serves on senior level intra- and intercorporate committees and working group. Manages the activities and provides leadership direction to the professional, technical, and support staff within the organization unit.

Qualification guidelines

Master's degree in an area of study relevant to this position and more than 4 years experience with a major law enforcement, intelligence, public service or private sector security organization; or bachelor's degree or international equivalent in an area of study relevant to this position and more than 10 years experience with a major law enforcement, intelligence, public, or private sector security organization. Has had exposure in the international security arena. Certification preferred.

Senior business unit security manager IV
Job Code 344

Job description

Works under consultative direction toward predetermined goals and objectives. Assignments are usually self-initiated. Determines and pursues courses of action necessary to obtain desired results, and makes recommendations and changes to departmental policies and procedures. Performs the full range of security functions such as inspections, identification of vulnerabilities, and assessment of risks. Makes recommendations of appropriate and required security measures, techniques, and methods to assure and improve the protection of personnel, activities, and facilities of the organization. Work is checked through consultation and agreement, rather than formal review of the supervisor. Develops and implements policies, procedures, standards, training, and methods for identifying and protecting information, personnel, property, facilities, operations, or material from unauthorized disclosure, misuse, theft, assault, vandalism, product tampering, espionage, sabotage, or loss. Reviews security project designs and contacts on-site progress assessments to insure design specifications meet the security needs. Performs security risk assessments based on vulnerability criteria to determine appropriate levels of protection and security necessary for the site. Recommends and coordinates the acquisition, installation, or replacement of equipment designed to increase efficiency of security operations at facilities. Assists in the evaluation of state-of-the-art products and techniques related to computer hardware and software. Receives and evaluates all security-related incidents and makes recommendations to preclude recurrence. Independently plans and conducts sensitive and complex security assessments and briefs senior management on the status of these investigations. Leads large-scale security inspections and risk assessments. Evaluates the latest products and techniques in communications and other technical equipment. Represents the organization in intra- and intercompany committees. Provides leadership to less experienced unit managers and unit personnel.

Qualification guidelines

Bachelor's degree in an area of study relevant to this position and more than 8 years experience with a major law enforcement, intelligence, public, or private sector security organization. Certification preferred.

Business unit security manager III

Job Code 345

Job description

Works under general supervision. Follows established procedures. Work is reviewed for soundness of technical judgment and overall adequacy. With guidance, performs the full range of security functions such as inspections, identification of vulnerabilities, assessment of risks and recommendation of appropriate and required security measures, and techniques and methods to assure and improve the protection of personnel, activities, and facilities of the organization. Participates in the development and implementation of policies, procedures, standards, training, and methods for identifying and protecting information, personnel, property, facilities, operations, or material from unauthorized disclosure, misuse, theft, assault, vandalism, product tampering, espionage, sabotage, or loss. Reviews security project designs and conducts on-site progress assessments to ensure that design specifications meet the security needs. Performs security risk assessments based on vulnerability criteria to determine appropriate levels of protection and security necessary for the site. Participates in the acquisition of new equipment designed to increase efficiency of security operations at facilities. Coordinates the installation or replacement of the facilities security equipment. Participates in the evaluation of the state-of-the-art products and techniques related to computer hardware and software. Conducts comprehensive review and analysis of facility security plans for compliance with existing policies and procedures. Receives and evaluates all security-related incidents and makes recommendations to preclude recurrence. Based on incidents, trends and surveys, recommends corrective action. Prepares written or narrative reports of facility assessment findings. May act as a lead person or technical expert on small to medium projects.

Qualification guidelines

Bachelor's degree in an area of study relevant to this position and more than 6 years experience with a major law enforcement, intelligence, public, or private sector security organization. Certification preferred.

Business unit security manager II

Job Code 346

Job description

Works under general supervision. Follows established procedures. Work is reviewed systematically through completion for adequacy in meeting objectives. With guidance, performs the full range of security functions such as inspections, identification of vulnerabilities, assessment of risks and recommendation of appropriate and required security measures, and techniques and methods to assure and improve the protection of personnel, activities, and facilities of the organization. Analyzes, advises, and evaluates security functions with effect to the development and implementation of policies, procedures, standards, training, and methods for identifying and protecting information, personnel, property, facilities, operations, or material from unauthorized disclosure, misuse, theft, assault, vandalism, product tampering, espionage, sabotage, or loss. Reviews security project designs and conducts on-site progress assessments to ensure that design specifications meet the security needs. Performs security risk assessments based on vulnerability criteria to determine appropriate levels of protection and security necessary for the site. Assists in recommending and coordinating the acquisition, installation, or replacement of equipment designed to increase the efficiency of security operations at facilities. Assists in the evaluation of the state-of-the-art products and techniques related to computer hardware and software. Works with business unit managers and employees in promoting and maintaining management initiatives to implement security objectives. Receives and evaluates all security-related incidents and makes recommendations to preclude recurrence. Based on incidents, trends, and surveys, recommends corrective action. Prepares written, narrative reports of facility assessment findings. Assists in developing and presenting security training programs. May act as a lead person or technical advisor on small projects.

Qualification guidelines

Bachelor's degree in an area of study relevant to this position and more than 4 years experience with a major law enforcement, intelligence, public, or private sector security organization. Certification preferred.

Business unit security manager I

Job Code 347

Job description

Works under close supervision. Performs tasks from detailed instructions and established procedures. Work is reviewed for soundness of technical judgment and for following the defined policies and procedures. Under direction of senior staff, observes and assists in the analysis, development, and implementation of policies, procedures, standards, training, and methods for identifying and protecting information, personnel, property, facilities, operations, or material from unauthorized disclosure, misuse, theft, assault, vandalism, product tampering, espionage, sabotage, or loss. Assists experienced security specialists and business unit managers in conducting security risk assessments, and assists in the evaluation of findings and development and recommendations for improvement or change. Participates in researching the application and evaluation of the state-of-the-art products and techniques related to computer hardware and software. Assists senior security specialists and business unit managers and employees in promoting and maintaining management initiatives to implement security objectives. Receives and tracks security-related incidents, and assists in recommendations to preclude recurrence. Prepares written or narrative reports of facility assessment findings.

Qualification guidelines

Bachelor's degree in an area of study relevant to this position and a minimum of 2 years progressive experience with a major law enforcement, intelligence, public, or private sector security organization. Certification preferred.

Manager, emergency preparedness/disaster recovery
Job Code 352

Job description

Plans, develops, and manages the corporate emergency preparedness/disaster recovery programs for the company under senior management direction. Responsible for the business strategies associated with the emergency preparedness/disaster recovery function within the organization. Accountable for overall planning, directing, and organizing activities of the programs, and ensure their effective operation. Implements policies, procedures, and systems required for maintaining and enhancing the overall emergency preparedness/disaster recovery mission. Oversees the architecture of recovery systems to include data systems, and data networks to ensure the integrity and security of all electronics data and data systems are adequately protected. This includes procedure writing; program planning; project design and scheduling; development and delivering training; and planning and conducting drills and exercises; designing, developing, and maintaining emergency response facilities and equipment. Designs, develops, and conducts drills and exercises. Plans, schedules, and conducts a wide range of very complex facility and/or site emergency preparedness/disaster recovery drills which could include emergency response training drills, medical drills, fire response drills, nuclear incident monitoring drills, and protective action drills. Determines the need for emergency plans changes and new procedures and ensures the appropriate government format and content are followed. Coordinate with state and local emergency management authorities. Maintains expert knowledge of the organization's processes and hazards, interfaces with engineering and operations staff to ensure appropriate development of a facility and/or site-specific hazard assessment and emergency classification procedures. Prepares technical reports based on the expert interpretation of analyzed data.

Qualification guidelines

Master's degree in studies relevant to this position and more than 6 years emergency management/disaster recovery experience with a major corporation and/or law enforcement, intelligence, public service, or private sector security organization; or a bachelor's degree in studies relevant to this position and more than 10 years emergency management/disaster recovery experience. Certification preferred.

Senior emergency preparedness specialist IV

Job Code 354

Job description

Works under consultative direction toward predetermined goals and objectives. Assignments are usually self-initiated. Determines and pursues courses of action necessary to obtain desired results. Exercises technical discretion within broadly defined practices and policies in selecting methods, techniques, and evaluation criterion for obtaining results. Oversees the design, development, and maintenance of the organization's emergency preparedness program. This could include procedure writing; program planning; project design and scheduling; development and delivering training; planning and conducting drills and exercises; and designing, developing, and maintaining emergency response facilities and equipment. Designs, develops, and conducts drills and exercises. May manage the scenario development portion of schedule. May act as the senior team leader to plan, schedule, and conduct a wide range of very complex facility and/or site emergency preparedness drills which could include emergency response training drills, medical drills, fire response drills, nuclear incident monitoring drills, and protective action drills. Determines the need for emergency plans changes and new procedures and ensures the appropriate government format and content are followed. May coordinate with state and local emergency management authorities. With expert knowledge of the organization's processes and hazards, interfaces with engineering and operations staff to ensure appropriate development of a facility and/or site-specific hazard assessment and emergency classification procedures. Prepares technical reports based on the expert interpretation of analyzed data. Provides leadership to less-experienced specialists and technicians through work as-assignments, monitoring schedules, and resolving problems. May act as a lead person or technical expert on projects.

Qualification guidelines

Bachelor's degree in an area of study relevant to this position and more than 8 years experience in emergency management with a law enforcement, public, or private sector security organization. Certification preferred.

Emergency preparedness specialist III
Job Code 355

Job description

Works under very general direction. Exercises reasonable latitude in determining technical objectives of assignments. Work is reviewed upon completion for adequacy in meeting objectives. Works on problems of diverse scope and complexity where analysis of data requires evaluation of identifiable factors. Uses technical discretion within generally defined practices and policies in selecting methods and techniques for obtaining solutions. Participates in designing, developing, and maintaining the organization's emergency preparedness program. This could include procedure writing; program planning; project design and scheduling; development and delivering training; planning and conducting drills and exercises; and designing, developing, and maintaining emergency response facilities and equipment. Conducts emergency preparedness drills and exercises. May oversee the scenario development portion of schedule. Assists in design and development of training lesson plans and conducts procedure training. May lead a project team to plan, schedule, and conduct a wide range of complex facility and/or site emergency preparedness drills which could include emergency response training drills, medical drills, fire response drills, nuclear incident monitoring drills, and protective action drills. Participates in identifying the need for emergency plan changes and new procedures and ensures that the appropriate government format and content are followed. Provides coordination with state and local emergency management authorities. With good working knowledge of the organization's processes and hazards, interfaces with engineering and operations staff to ensure appropriate development of a facility and/or site-specific hazard assessment and emergency classification procedures. May provide leadership to less-experienced specialists and to technicians through work assignments, monitoring schedules and resolving problems. May also act as lead person or technical expert on small to medium projects.

Qualification guidelines

Bachelor's degree in an area of study relevant to this position and more than 6 years experience in emergency management with a law enforcement, public, or private sector security organization. Certification preferred.

Senior nuclear accountability specialist IV

Job Code 364

Job description

Works under consultative direction toward predetermined goals and objectives. Assignments are usually self-initiated. Determines and pursues courses of action necessary to obtain desired results, and makes recommendations and changes to departmental policies and procedures. Work is checked through consultation and agreement, rather than formal review of the supervisor. Provides nuclear accountability services and support to include comprehensive analysis and reporting of nuclear inventory data. Identifies inventory issues and makes recommendations for their resolution. Monitors, reconciles, and enhances financial systems. Interprets nuclear data in accordance with general accepted accounting principles. Prepares comprehensive accounting and inventory utilizing various nuclear material inventory systems. Specifies requirements for business applications, conducts feasibility and cost benefits, develops and executes software acceptance testing, and organizes and directs implementations. Coordinates input of nuclear inventory data in accordance with accounting cycle, including preparation and review of inventory statements. Analyzes nuclear materials inventory transactions and prepares monthly material balance reports, inventory statements, and inventory related financial statements. Conducts reviews of nuclear processes, recommends and establishes inventory models that accurately reflect nuclear movements and locations. Monitors, analyzes, and corrects variances between site nuclear material inventory records and external databases. Analyzes, interprets, and applies statistical inventory models to determine significance of inventory variances. Interprets and identifies nuclear transactions to ensure good business practices and adherence to domestic and international policies on accounting for nuclear materials. Researches and interprets federal and international regulations for internationally safeguarded, strategic reserve, tritium stockpile, spent nuclear fuel, and set aside nuclear material inventories. Provides leadership to less-experienced nuclear accountability specialists and technicians.

Qualification guidelines

Bachelor's degree in an area of study relevant to this position and more than 8 years experience in emergency management with a law enforcement, or public or private sector security organization. Certification preferred.

Nuclear accountabilities specialist III

Job Code 365

Job description

Works under very general direction. Exercises reasonable latitude in determining nuclear accountability techniques to accomplish objectives. Work is reviewed upon completion for adequacy in meeting objectives. Provides nuclear accountability services and support to include analyzing and reporting of nuclear inventory data. Monitors and reconciles nuclear material accounts. Prepares inventory statements and transactions, maintains ledgers, accounts and tables; coordination of shipments and receipts of nuclear material; and coordinates input of inventory data in accordance with generally accepted accounting principles. Coordinates input of nuclear inventory data in accordance with accounting cycles, which includes preparation and review of inventory statements. Conducts audits and appraisals of selected nuclear material accounting functions. Analyzes nuclear materials inventory transactions and prepares monthly material balance reports, inventory statements, and inventory related financial statements. Monitors, analyzes, and corrects variances between site nuclear material inventory records and external databases. Analyzes, interprets, and applies statistical inventory models to determine significance of inventory variances. Interprets and identifies nuclear transactions to ensure good business practices and adherence to domestic and international policies on accounting for nuclear materials. Researches and interprets federal and international regulations for internationally safeguarded, strategic reserve, tritium stockpile, spent nuclear fuel, and set aside nuclear material inventories. Provides leadership to less-experienced nuclear accountability specialists and technicians.

Qualification guidelines

Bachelor's degree in an area of study relevant to this position and more than 6 years experience in emergency management with a law enforcement, public, or private sector security organization. Certification preferred.

Senior manager, product protection security
Job Code 368

Job description

Plans, develops, and directs the product protection security function within the organization to ensure its effective operation based on predetermined goals and objectives under executive management direction. Implements product protection projects as part of the core mission of the Global Product Protection organization taking responsibility for devising the solution set, identifying the projects, designing and managing the project plan, establishing proof of concept, and then assisting the organization in implementing and sustaining the operational aspects of the programs. Responsible for managing the anti-illicit trade investigations, including directing investigations on illegal product and packaging manufactures. Develops, manages, and deploys processes and measures for identifying potential high-risk products and vulnerable channels of distribution in the United States and if applicable, worldwide markets. Ensures effective coordination of product protection technologies within the business processes and goals; provides market monitoring analysis of the supply chain transactions and practices. Align product protection priorities and activities across company functions. Responsible for affecting and maintaining liaison with government authorities on illicit trade activities. Manages the development of the legal and intellectual property, supply chain security and forensics and technology programs that support the operation of product protection. Foster and maintain relationships with external suppliers and consultants to develop and promote products and processes in the area of product protection. Develops and implements product protection programs and processes into the companies or organizations in order to assure sustainable product protection results and best practices. Researches, assesses, and manages technologies that will help reduce counterfeiting and illegal diversion for the company. Responsible for the selecting and developing of key security personnel for the product protection function of the organization. Responsible for submitting and maintaining the group's budget.

Qualification guidelines

Master's degree or international equivalent in an area of study relevant to this position and more than 10 years experience with a major law enforcement, public service, or private sector security organization; or bachelor's degree or international equivalent in an area of study relevant to this position and more than 12 years experience with a major law enforcement, public, or private sector security organization. Hands-on operational experience in litigation-related investigations, including antipiracy and anticounterfeiting operations. CPP, PCI (professional certified investigator), and CFE preferred.

Manager, product protection security
Job Code 369

Job description

Plans, develops, and directs the product protection security function under senior management direction. Responsible for the business strategies associated with product protection security function within the organization. Initiates, manages, and successfully resolve investigations of alleged and/or confirmed counterfeiting, tampering, and diversion of company products. Manages the comprehensive intellectual property infringement policy and strategy to minimize any losses. Reviews and reports risk assessments to identify threats to security of information, systems, and computing assets throughout the company in regard to product protection. Manages and establishes an effective reporting and tracking system for processing of complaints, investigation, and enforcement actions. Manages anticounterfeiting initiatives and tracking methodologies. Coordinates field investigations of product counterfeiting, gray-market and related incidents and interface with law enforcement and prosecutors. Manages and maintains a network of key relationships including company, professional product protection management, law enforcement, and outside contacts. Manages the formation and implementation of corporate product protection policies with other product protection peers within the company. Develop strategies on enhancing product protection technologies and processes that identify and stop illegal activities while recouping lost revenue. Manages key collaboration with affiliates to implement consistent standards, programs, assessments, and procedures for the product security with consideration for developing relationships with supply chain partners. Researches and manages technologies that will help reduce counterfeiting and illegal diversion for the company. Ensures effective information sharing and coordination within operating units in regard to product protection strategies and guidelines. Develops, trains, and directs product security personal within the organization.

Qualification guidelines

Master's degree or international equivalent in an area of study relevant to this position and more than 7 years experience with a major law enforcement, intelligence, public service, or private sector security organization; or bachelor's degree or international equivalent in an area of study relevant to this position and more than 10 years experience with a major law enforcement, intelligence, public, or private sector security organization. Hands-on operational experience in litigation-related investigations, including antipiracy and anticounterfeiting operations. CPP, PCI, and CFE preferred.

Senior product protection security specialist IV

Job Code 370

Job description

Works under consultative direction toward predetermined goals and objectives. Assignments are usually self-initiated. Determines and pursues courses of action necessary to obtain desired results, and makes recommendations and changes to departmental policies and procedures. Initiates and implements the business strategies associated with product protection security function within the organization. Tracks, organizes, and implements the comprehensive intellectual property infringements policy and strategy to minimize any losses. May review and report risk assessments to identify threats to security of information, systems, and computing assets throughout the company in regard to product protection. Align product protection policies and procedures across the organization and externally with commercial partners. Researches and recommends technologies that will help reduce counterfeiting and illegal activities for the company's products. Works with vendors for current and applicable anticounterfeiting technologies and processes designed to mitigate product losses. Maintains liaison contacts within the industry, law enforcement, government, and regulatory agencies to maintain knowledge of and provide recommendations for strategic response to possible litigation, trends, external risks, and new technology related to product security. Use appropriate investigative technologies and processes to achieve maximum efficiencies and effectiveness. Produces written statements and reports for evidential purposes. Works with the intellectual property legal team to establish a legal framework and best practice to follow for the successful prosecution of copyright infringement offenders. Supports forensic needs and activities for security incident management and investigations. May assist with and participate in the development and implementation of a product protection security plan that assesses current threats and vulnerabilities, identifies protection goals, objectives, and metrics consistent with corporate strategic objectives, and details the efficient and cost-effective utilization of security resources. Prepares and disseminates detailed investigation and risk trending/analysis reports as required. Provides leadership to less experienced product protection specialists and technicians.

Qualification guidelines

Master's degree or international equivalent in an area of study relevant to this position and more than 4 years experience with a major law enforcement, intelligence, public service, or private sector security organization; or bachelor's degree or international equivalent in an area of study relevant to this position and more than 8 years experience with a major law enforcement, intelligence, public, or private sector security organization. Hands-on operational experience in litigation-related investigations, including antipiracy and anticounterfeiting operations. CPP, PCI, and CFE preferred.

Product protection security specialist III
Job Code 371

Job description

Works under general direction. Exercises reasonable latitude in determining product protection security techniques to accomplish objectives. Work is reviewed upon completion for adequacy in meeting objectives. Participates in the implementation of business strategies associated with product protection security function within the organization. Tracks, organizes, and implements the comprehensive intellectual property infringement policy and strategy to minimize any losses. May review and report risk assessments to identify threats to security of information, systems, and computing assets throughout the company in regard to product protection. Implements product protection policies and procedures across the organization and external commercial partners. Recommends technologies that will help reduce counterfeiting and illegal activities for the company's products. Works with vendors for current and applicable anticounterfeiting technologies and processes designed to mitigate product losses. Assists in conducting quality control audits to evaluate product protection security standards and performance levels ensuring uniformity and effectiveness of product protection technologies and procedures. Conducts vulnerability exercises to identify and reduce exposures. Uses appropriate investigative technologies and processes to achieve maximum efficiencies and effectiveness. Maintains liaison with customs/law enforcement/judicial agencies to assist the corporation pursuing matters through the criminal justice system. May work with vendors for current and applicable anticounterfeiting technologies and processes designed to mitigate product losses. Produces written statements and reports for evidential purposes. Identifies product security risks to company supply chains, and recommend appropriate product security protocols to mitigate product risk. Assists in security due diligence assessments on potential business partners such as wholesalers, distributors, brokers, or other organizational critical functions. Participates in the dissemination of detailed investigation and risk trending/analysis reports as required. Provides input to the intellectual property legal team to establish a legal framework and best practice to follow for the successful prosecution of copyright infringement offenders.

Qualification guidelines

Bachelor's degree or an international equivalent in an area of study relevant to this position and more than 6 years experience with a major law enforcement, intelligence, public service, or private sector security organization. Hands-on operational experience in litigation related investigations, including antipiracy and anticounterfeiting operations. CPP, PCI, and CFE preferred.

Product protection security specialist II

Job Code 372

Job description

Works under general supervision. Work is reviewed systematically through completion for adequacy in meeting objectives. Work is reviewed upon completion for adequacy in meeting objectives. Product protection work is assigned by management. Maintains and follows the comprehensive intellectual property infringement policy and strategy to minimize any losses. With management direction, may conduct risk assessments to identify threats to security of information, systems, and computing assets throughout the company in regard to product protection. Works within product protection policies and procedures across the organization and externally with commercial partners. Monitors and investigates alleged trademark infringements to include unauthorized commercial use of company products, including counterfeiting of products. Works to compile facts and gather evidence for use in civil and criminal matters. Works within established company protocols to manage and streamline activities surrounding the recovery of confiscated product. Assists in managing a relational database designed to analyze, report, and document contraband activities, to include incident reports and findings. May act as a liaison with company organizations in terms of product protection procedures and interpretation of policies. May assist in utilizing Internet and computer-related investigations to gather competitive intelligence on black market activities involving company products. Supports the authentication process for suspected counterfeit company products, and assists on other antipiracy/infringement matters. Assists in preparing and maintaining documentation required by outside authorities and communication with internal departments. Assists in the support on product security litigations, including preparing documentation/evidence, coordinates with lawyers and authorities, maintaining records, and follow-up on litigation process. Maintains excellent working relationships with the relevant law enforcement agencies, supporting agencies, and organizations. Works with outside vendors.

Qualification guidelines

Bachelor's degree in an area of study relevant to this position and more than 4 years experience with a major law enforcement, intelligence, public, or private sector security organization. Operational experience in litigation-related investigations, including antipiracy and anticounterfeiting operations preferred. CPP, PCI, and CFE preferred.

Product protection security specialist I
Job Code 373

Job description

Works under close supervision. The product protection caseload is assigned by management or senior specialists. Performs tasks from detailed instructions and established procedures. Work is reviewed for soundness of established product protection techniques and for following the defined policies and procedures. Based on product protection policy, follows the comprehensive intellectual property infringement policy and strategy to minimize any losses. Assists higher-level product protection specialists as they monitor and investigate alleged trademark infringements to include unauthorized commercial use of company products, including counterfeiting of products. Assists in compiling facts and gathers evidence for use in civil and criminal matters. Follows established company protocols to manage and streamline activities surrounding the recovery of confiscated product. Assists in maintaining an accurate, up-to-date case files and database. May assist in compiling facts and gather evidence for use in civil and criminal matters as it relates to the organizations' product protection policies. Supports the management of a relational database designed to analyze, report, and document contraband activities to include incident reports and findings. Supports the authentication process for suspected counterfeit company products, and assists in other antipiracy/infringement matters. With senior direction, monitors and investigates alleged trademark infringements. Support senior product protection specialists in defined protocols in regard to product protection where work and methodologies are evaluated as to technical soundness, appropriateness, and effectiveness in meeting operational goals and objectives.

Qualification guidelines

Bachelor's degree in an area of study relevant to this position and more than 2 years experience with a major law enforcement, intelligence, public, or private sector security organization. CPP, PCI, or CFE preferred.

Security clearance specialist II

Job Code 386

Job description

Works under general supervision and follows established procedures. Work is reviewed for soundness of technical judgment and overall adequacy. Reviews electronic security clearance applications for completeness and enters employee security data into the government's Electronic Personnel Security Questionnaire software program for transmittal to the Defense Security Service. Grants security clearance to personnel in the organization as needed. Safeguards classified materials and conducts periodic inspection and inventory of specific project's classified status. Compiles information of a sensitive and confidential nature regarding senior management and the organization for government reporting. Meets with Department of Energy (DOE) representatives and/or Defense Security Service agents regarding project issues, personnel clearance, cleared facilities, and other security matters. Provides management with interpretation of the *National Industrial Security Program Operating Manual* to ensure compliance with government projects and updates the organization's standard practice procedures when appropriate. Works closely with management in reviewing government contract requirements.

Qualification guidelines

Bachelor's degree in an area of study relevant to this position and more than 4 years experience in a law enforcement, public, or private sector security organization. Certification preferred.

Physical security systems specialist III
Job Code 392

Job description

Works under very limited direction. Exercises reasonable latitude in determining the most appropriate physical security techniques to accomplish objectives. Work is reviewed upon completion for adequacy in meeting objectives. With limited guidance, plans and recommends to the management, the physical security systems and service requirements for the company. Responsible for the coordination, installation, upgrade, and conversion or servicing of alarm systems, access controls, video cameras, burglary, radio systems, and all other types of physical security equipment. Defines physical security system standards, policies, required upgrades, maintenance, and day-to-day management of all security systems through system integrators or internal resources. Directs external relationships to ensure the viability of all physical security systems, legacy and new, with the goal of minimal business disruption as the result of failed or improperly configured systems. Implements technology solutions aligned with corporate security strategy and budget guidelines. Maintains an in-depth knowledge of the state-of-the-art security equipment standards and technology encompassing all physical security products. Provides system solutions to specific security concerns identified through customer requests and security audits. Develops and maintains operational processes to ensure security standards are maintained. Develops and administers processes for annual audits for various access control systems. Acts as a primary contact for security system emergency issues. Provides product research, feasibility studies, project planning, tracking, and quality assurance and overall vendor communication and management. Acts as a primary contact for physical security system emergency management. Advises and assists in annual security systems budgeting process.

Qualification guidelines

Bachelor's degree in an area of study relevant to this position and more than 6 years experience with physical security systems and security software. Knowledge and experience in working with information technology security application and practices. Certification preferred.

Physical security systems specialist II

Job Code 393

Job description

Work is performed under general supervision. Follows established procedures. Work is reviewed systematically through completion for adequacy in meeting objectives. With guidance, assists in the planning of the physical security systems and service requirements for the company. Responsible for maintaining, coordinating, installing, upgrading, converting, or servicing of alarm systems, access controls, video cameras, burglary, radio systems, and all other types of physical security equipment. Participates in the definition of physical security system standards, required upgrades, maintenance, and day-to-day operation of all security systems through system integrators or internal resources. Interacts with external relationships to ensure the viability of security systems, legacy and new, with the goal of minimal business disruption as the result of failed or improperly configured systems. Assists in the implementation of technology solutions aligned with corporate security goals and budget guidelines. Maintains an in-depth knowledge of the state-of-the-art security equipment standards and technology encompassing all physical security products. Recommends to management system solutions to specific security concerns identified through customer requests and security audits. Performs operational processes to ensure security standards are maintained. Administers processes for annual audits for various access control systems. Acts as a primary contact for physical security system emergency issues. Provides product research, feasibility studies, project planning, tracking, and quality assurance and overall vendor communication and management. May act as a primary contact for physical security system emergency management. Assists in annual security systems budgeting process.

Qualification guidelines

Bachelor's degree in an area of study relevant to this position and more than 4 years experience with physical security systems and security software. Knowledge and experience in working with information technology security application and practices. Certification preferred.

Senior manager, product protection programs
Job Code 401

Job description

Work is performed under general supervision. Follows established procedures. Work is reviewed systematically through completion for adequacy in meeting objectives. With guidance, assists in the planning of the physical security systems and service requirements for the company. Responsible for maintaining, coordinating, installing, upgrading, converting, or servicing of alarm systems, access controls, video cameras, burglary, radio systems, and all other types of physical security equipment. Participates in the definition of physical security system standards, required upgrades, maintenance, and day-to-day operation of all security systems through system integrators or internal resources. Interacts with external relationships to ensure the viability of security systems, legacy and new, with the goal of minimal business disruption as the result of failed or improperly configured systems. Assists in the implementation of technology solutions aligned with corporate security goals and budget guidelines. Maintains an in-depth knowledge of the state-of-the-art security equipment standards and technology encompassing all physical security products. Recommends to management system solutions to specific security concerns identified through customer requests and security audits. Performs operational processes to ensure security standards are maintained. Administers processes for annual audits for various access control systems. Acts as a primary contact for physical security system emergency issues. Provides product research, feasibility studies, project planning, tracking, and quality assurance and overall vendor communication and management. May act as a primary contact for physical security system emergency management. Assists in annual security systems budgeting process.

Qualification guidelines

Bachelor's degree in an area of study relevant to this position and more than 4 years experience with physical security systems and security software. Knowledge and experience in working with information technology security application and practices. Certification preferred.

Manager, corporate security programs

Job Code 402

Job description

Plans, develops, and manages the corporate programs for the security function under senior management direction. Programs include workplace violence, technical abuse, and organizational integrity, which encompass business and employee conduct, compliance, ethics, and privacy. Develops and documents standards of measurement of the efficiency and effectiveness of these programs. Plans, develops, and presents organization-wide policies on procedures, guidance for personnel to implement. Coordinates inspections, reporting, and documenting of emergency response activities of relevant programs. Monitors and reports noncompliance of security breeches to appropriate department heads. Develops employee training and awareness programs and manages development campaigns. Manages day-to-day operation of business and employee conduct program, including hotline call intake, analysis, routing, response, reporting, and follow-up. Coordinates development and maintenance of database to track and analyze inappropriate communications that insinuate or allege a grievance or personal threat to executives, employees, or other individuals associated with the organization. Coordinates the development, implementation, and documentation of corporate security program records. Assists security staff in providing expertise and procedural guidance to management and staff of operating units. Interacts with management and human resources staff in intervention procedures related to potential workplace violence cases. Identifies, provides technical expertise, evaluates content and makes recommendations on incorporating all facets of corporate programs into the business operation. Identifies and develops resource requirements for corporate program goals and objectives. Manages the activities and provides leadership direction to the professional, technical, and support staff within the organization unit.

Qualification guidelines

Bachelor's degree in an area of study relevant to this position and more than 10 years experience with a major law enforcement, intelligence, public, or private sector security organization. Certification preferred.

Manager, security systems and training
Job Code 412

Job description

Plans and directs the organization's security computer systems, data repositories, and technology tools under senior management direction. Implements technology solutions and services for security website, personnel identification, incident reporting, case management, and system validation. Serves as a leading technical expert on complex security equipment and techniques. Oversees technical functions in support of security and investigative operations. Directs the evaluation of state-of-the-art products and techniques related to computer hardware and software. Provides expertise of their use, recommends equipment, and adapts changes to computer technologies. Provides technical advise, guidance, and recommendations regarding security programs and awareness media. Implements staff, employee, and facility training programs, coordinates and develops communication plans, documented guidelines/manuals, and customer satisfaction surveys. Designs communication plans by documenting guidelines, brochures, surveys in on-line network, and automated self-assessment formats. Acquires and coordinates training programs by adapting or translating materials from a variety of recognized sources. Analyzes departmental financial performance results and prepares expense and capital budget worksheets. Ensures successful program results and value contributions through interpersonal contact with peers and senior management. Manages the activities and provides leadership direction to the professional, technical, and support staff within the organization unit.

Qualification guidelines

Bachelor's degree in computer science or other studies relevant to this position and more than 10 years experience with a major law enforcement, intelligence, public, or private sector security organization. Has had some exposure in the international security arena. CISSP preferred and certified security training specialist (CSTS) preferred.

Senior security training and awareness specialist IV

Job Code 414

Job description

Works under consultative direction toward predetermined goals and objectives. Assignments are usually self-initiated. Determines and pursues courses of action necessary to obtain desired results, and makes recommendations and changes to departmental policies and procedures. Work is checked through consultation and agreement, rather than formal review of the supervisor. Acts as a senior member of a team to implement technology solutions and services for security website, personnel identification, incident reporting, case management, and system validation. Administer presentation of initial or new hire security briefing, annual refresher, and termination briefings for the organization. Accountable for automated administrative system to ensure tracking of briefing attendance. Employs a variety of awareness media to keep managers and employees abreast of latest information, personnel, and technical security policies, procedures, trends, and issues. Communicates with line and staff personnel on potential threats to work environment. Through appropriate media devices, ensures line and staff personnel are kept abreast of potential threats, vulnerabilities, and countermeasures germane to work environment. Participates in local, regional, and national workshops and seminars related to security education and awareness. Keeps abreast of hardware and software security applications and their use in the current operating environment. Provides input for the development of new security-related orders, manuals, and guides and delivers presentations to organization staff. Provides leadership to less experienced security awareness/training specialists and technicians.

Qualification guidelines

Bachelor's degree in an area of study relevant to this position and more than 8 years experience in emergency management with a law enforcement, public, or private sector security organization. CSTS preferred.

Security training and awareness specialist III
Job Code 415

Job description
Works under very general direction. Exercises reasonable latitude in determining security communication/awareness techniques to accomplish objectives. Work is reviewed upon completion for adequacy in meeting objectives. Works as a team member to implement technology solutions and services for security website, personnel identification, incident reporting, case management, and system validation. Administer presentation of initial or new hire security briefing, annual refresher, and termination briefings for the organization. Accountable for automated administrative system to ensure tracking of briefing attendance. Employs a variety of awareness media to keep managers and employees abreast of latest information, personnel, and technical security policies, procedures, trends, and issues. Communicates with line and staff personnel on potential threats to work environment. Through appropriate media devices, ensures line and staff personnel are kept abreast of potential threats, vulnerabilities, and countermeasures germane to work environment. Participates in local, regional, and national workshops and seminars related to security education and awareness. Keeps abreast of hardware and software security applications and their use in the current operating environment. Provides input for the development of new security-related orders, manuals, and guides and delivers presentations to organization staff. Provides leadership to less-experienced security awareness/training specialists and technicians.

Qualification guidelines
Bachelor's degree in an area of study relevant to this position and more than 6 years experience in emergency management with a law enforcement, public, or private sector security organization. CSTS preferred.

Manager, classified security projects
Job Code 422

Job description

Plans and directs the classified security projects function under senior management direction. The position is accountable for initiating and administering a classified security program that will enable the organization to pursue and perform work on government-classified contracts. Responsible for the organization's classification, export control (EC), and classified matter protection and control (CMPC) programs in order to ensure that all subcontractor firms are in compliance with applicable government orders, regulations, laws, and treaties. Develops policies and procedures that govern the programs and ensure compliance of all subcontract companies via management assessment. Serves as the organization's classification, EC, and CMPC authority, adjudicate and establishes the organization's position on all related issues. Directs the review of classified records holdings. Oversees and conducts reviews for classified and sensitive unclassified information (may include unclassified controlled nuclear information and export controlled information) within documents or matter intended for widespread dissemination of public release. Provides review support in a timely manner for all public request of documents. Directly interacts with DOE and other government agencies on all matters related to classified matters. Ensures the proper identification, markings, and controls of nuclear-related equipment and materials held by the organization as defined by the DOE. Participates in all activities related to the declassifying and downgrading classified matter. Briefs all levels of management on classification issues and classification requirements for sensitive technologies and processes. Manages the activities and provides leadership direction to the professional, technical, and support staff within the organization unit.

Qualification guidelines

Bachelor's degree in an area of study relevant to this position and more than 10 years experience with classification and EC work in a government facility/agency or private sector security organization. Certification preferred.

Senior classified security specialist IV

Job Code 424

Job description

Works under consultative direction toward predetermined goals and objectives. Assignments are usually self-initiated. Determines and pursues courses of action necessary to obtain desired results. Exercises technical discretion within broadly defined practices and policies in selecting methods, techniques, and evaluation criterion for obtaining results. Provides technical support regarding the classified security program that will enable the organization to pursue and perform work on government-classified contracts. Ensures proper classification and subsequent protection of documents, computer systems, and any nuclear-related items of importance to national security, originated or controlled by the organization and subcontractors prior to release of such items for widespread distribution and public release. Monitors the organization's classification, EC, and CMPC programs in order to ensure that all subcontractor firms are in compliance with applicable government orders, regulations, laws, and treaties. Participates in developing policies and procedures that govern the programs and ensure compliance of all subcontract companies via management assessment. Participates in the review of classified records holdings. Oversees and conducts reviews for classified and sensitive unclassified information (may include unclassified controlled nuclear information and export controlled information) within documents or matter intended for widespread dissemination of public release. Interacts with DOE and other government agencies on all matters related to classified matters. Develops and implements training and certification programs. Participates in all activities related to the declassifying and downgrading classified matter. Briefs all levels of management on classification issues and classification requirements for sensitive technologies and processes. Prepares technical reports based on the expert interpretation of analyzed data. Provides leadership to less experienced specialists and to technicians. May act as a lead person or technical expert on projects.

Qualification guidelines

Bachelor's degree in an area of study relevant to this position and more than 8 years experience with classification and EC work in a government facility/agency or private sector security organization. Certification preferred.

Classified security specialist III

Job Code 425

Job description

Works under general supervision and follows established procedures. Work is reviewed for soundness of technical judgment and overall adequacy. Provides technical support regarding the classified security program that will enable the organization to pursue and perform work on government-classified contracts. Conducts reviews for classified and sensitive unclassified information (may include unclassified controlled nuclear information and export controlled information) within documents or matter intended for widespread dissemination of public release. Reviews proper classification and subsequent protection of documents, computer systems, and any nuclear-related items of importance to national security, originated or controlled by the organization and subcontractors prior to release of such items for widespread distribution and public release. Participates in monitoring the organization's classification, EC, and CMPC programs in order to ensure that all subcontractor firms are in compliance with applicable government orders, regulations, laws, and treaties. Assists in developing policies and procedures that govern the programs and ensure compliance of all subcontract companies via management assessment. Participates in the review of classified record holdings. Provides review support in a timely manner for all public request of documents. Interacts with DOE and other government agencies on all matters related to classified matters. Assists in developing and implementing training and certification programs. Participates in all activities related to the declassifying and downgrading classified matter. May assist in preparing technical reports based on the expert interpretation of analyzed data. May provide leadership to less-experienced specialists and to technicians through work assignments, monitoring schedules, and resolving problems. May act as a lead person or technical expert on small projects.

Qualification guidelines

Bachelor's degree in an area of study relevant to this position and more than 6 years experience with classification and EC work in a government facility/agency or private sector security organization. Certification preferred.

Manager, protective forces, armed/unarmed
Job Code 432

Job description

Plans, develops, and manages the corporate protective force programs security function under senior management direction. This position would have armed and unarmed guard force accountabilities. Responsible for the development of an efficient and safe operation of the organization's protective force operations. Manages the development and implementation of access and perimeter control operational procedures, conveying and verifying security requirements. Develops and manages corrective actions and upgrades to physical and technical security posture of the company. Identifies and recommends electronic access control equipment designed to detect unauthorized entry into facilities or property. Monitors performance and assignments of personnel and makes sporadic inspections to insure they are properly equipped, trained, and fulfilling their duties in compliance with company policies. Directs investigations related to accidents, arbitrations, and grievances as they occur, and institutes policy to prevent a recurrence. Directs personnel responsible for electronic and physical security systems, evaluates performance, and develops process and procedures to minimize risks. Monitors and directs emergency response operational plans and related activities as required. Coordinates security requirements and participates in planning of various on-site construction projects. Coordinates protective force administrative and operational matters with management, union officials, local law enforcement and client/customers to ensure continuity of operations. Manages the activities and provides leadership direction to the professional, technical, and support staff within the organization unit.

Qualification guidelines

Bachelor's degree in an area of study relevant to this position and more than 10 years experience in the armed forces security, military police, or with a major law enforcement, public, or private sector security organization. Must meet any physical requirements for defensive combat protective personnel. Also must qualify with weapons and have a background, which would not preclude a security clearance granted. CPP preferred.

Officer in charge, protective forces, armed

Job Code 433

Job description

Under general direction, supervises the personnel engaged in the protective forces function for the company. This position would have armed guard force accountabilities. Supervises the day-to-day shift operations of the department. Supervises the equipment used by personnel, investigates unusual incidents, and directs activities at emergencies. Assists in the development and implementation of access and perimeter control operational procedures, conveying and verifying security requirements. Implements corrective actions and upgrades to physical and technical security posture of the company. Identifies and recommends electronic access control equipment designed to detect unauthorized entry into facilities or property. Supervises assigned personnel in guard areas, initiate corrective actions, and completes daily activity reports. Directs personnel responsible for electronic and physical security systems, evaluates performance, and develops process and procedures to minimize risks. Ensures safety of personnel by checking and monitoring of all equipment in guard areas. Updates post orders, accounts for security seals, and supervises vehicle inspections. Participates in emergency response operational plans and related activities as required. Coordinates security requirements and participates in security planning of various on-site construction projects. Participates in protective force administrative and operational matters with management, union officials, local law enforcement, and client/customers to ensure continuity of operations. When necessary, supervises the handling of demonstrators and perpetrators. Supervises the activities and provides leadership direction to the professional, technical, and support staff within the organization unit.

Qualification guidelines

High school diploma or equivalent and more than 8 years progressive experience in the armed forces security, military police, or with a law enforcement, public, or private sector security organization. Must meet any physical requirements for defensive combat protective personnel. Also must qualify with weapons and have a background, which would not preclude a security clearance granted. CPP preferred.

Security officer 3, armed

Job Code 437

Job description

Under general supervision performs assigned tasks from detailed instructions. Protects the organization's physical assets by maintaining and safeguarding the physical perimeter, exterior, and interior perimeters of the facility. Patrols and protects the facilities by foot and/or vehicle to detect or prevent illegal/unauthorized activities. Provides security protection for all organizational facilities, classified material, and personnel within areas of responsibility to preclude unauthorized access, conversion, theft, or intentional destruction. Reports/responds to unusual or emergency situations, using the appropriate degree of physical force, and/or weaponry as situation dictates. Control personnel and vehicular ingress/egress into and exiting controlled secure areas. Be alert for potential security, property, or safety concerns and initiate the appropriate actions. Performs escort duties as appropriate. Prevents/reports all violations of security and safety rules and regulations. Responds to protective alarm signals or other unusual/suspicious activities. Maintains proficiency with all assigned weapons as required. Acts as a lead security officer to ensure safety of personnel by checking and monitoring of all equipment in guard areas. Tracks and updates post orders, accounts for security seals, and supervises vehicle inspections. Maintains an in-depth knowledge of all security orders, written and oral, pertaining to assigned duties as well as working knowledge of applicable federal/state laws. When necessary, assists in supervising the handling of demonstrators and perpetrators. Participates in a variety of training activities/programs designed to assure employees are capable of fulfilling their emergency response duties. Acts as a lead guard when required.

Qualification guidelines

High school diploma or equivalent and more than 6 years progressive experience in the armed forces security, military police, or with a law enforcement, public, or private sector security organization. Must meet any physical requirements for defensive combat protective personnel. Also must qualify with weapons and have a background, which would not preclude a security clearance granted. Must maintain a valid state driver's license. Must be able to perform duties wearing personal protective equipment.

Security officer 2, armed

Job Code 438

Job description

Under direct supervision performs assigned tasks from detailed instructions, established policies, and procedures. Protects the organization's physical assets by maintaining and safeguarding the physical perimeter, exterior, and interior perimeters of the facility. Patrols and protects the facilities by foot and/or vehicle to detect or prevent illegal/unauthorized activities. Provides security protection for all organizational facilities, classified material, and personnel within areas of responsibility to preclude unauthorized access, conversion, theft, or intentional destruction. Reports/responds to unusual or emergency situations, using the appropriate degree of physical force and/or weaponry as situation dictates. Control personnel and vehicular ingress/egress into and exiting controlled secure areas. Be alert for potential security, property or safety concerns, and initiate the appropriate actions. Perform escort duties as appropriate. Prevent/report all violations of security and safety rules and regulations. Respond to protective alarm signals or other unusual/suspicious activities. Maintain proficiency with all assigned weapons as required. Maintains an in-depth knowledge of all security orders, written and oral, pertaining to assigned duties as well as working knowledge of applicable federal/state laws.

Qualification guidelines

High school diploma or equivalent and more than 3 years progressive experience in the armed forces security, military police, or with a law enforcement, public, or private sector security organization. Must meet any physical requirements for defensive combat protective personnel. Also must qualify with weapons and have a background, which would not preclude a security clearance granted. Must maintain a valid state driver's license. Must be able to perform duties wearing personal protective equipment.

Security officer 1, armed

Job Code 439

Job description

Under immediate supervision performs routine, assigned tasks from detailed instructions, established policies, and procedures. Assists in the protection of the organization's physical assets by maintaining and safeguarding the physical perimeter, exterior, and interior perimeters of the facility. Assists in patrolling and protecting the facilities by foot and/or vehicle to detect or prevent illegal/unauthorized activities. Provides security protection for all organizational facilities and personnel within areas of responsibility to preclude unauthorized access, theft, or intentional destruction. With a senior security officer, responds to unusual or emergency situations using the appropriate degree of physical force and/or weaponry as situation dictates. Assists in the controlling of personnel and vehicular ingress/egress into and exiting controlled secure areas. Be alert for potential security, property, or safety concerns and initiate the appropriate actions by notifying senior personnel. Perform escort duties as appropriate. With direct supervision of a senior security officer, responds to protective alarm signals or other unusual/suspicious activities. Maintain proficiency with all assigned weapons as required.

Qualification guidelines

High school diploma or equivalent and a minimum of 2 year of progressive experience in the armed forces security, military police, or with a law enforcement, public, or private sector security organization. Must meet any physical requirements for defensive combat protective personnel. Also must qualify with weapons and have a background, which would not preclude a security clearance granted. Must maintain a valid state driver's license. Must be able to perform duties wearing personal protective equipment.

Manager, physical security, unarmed

Job Code 442

Job description

Plans, develops, and manages the corporate physical security program under senior management direction. Responsible for the development of an efficient and safe operation of the organization's physical security operations. Manages the development and implementation of access and perimeter control operational procedures, conveying and verifying security requirements. Manages the loss prevention and detection services and enforces administrative procedures. Develops and manages corrective actions to upgrade the physical and technical posture of the site. Manages the development and enhancements of security inspections procedures to prevent safety hazards, and ensures the proper procedures are followed. Acts as a liaison to field operations in the areas of design and implementation of physical security systems. Identifies and recommends electronic access control equipment designed to detect unauthorized entry into facilities or property. Monitors performance and assignments of personnel and makes sporadic inspections to insure they are properly equipped, trained, and fulfilling their duties in compliance with organization policies. Directs personnel responsible for electronic and physical security systems, evaluates performance, and develops process and procedures to minimize risks. Monitors and directs emergency response operational plans and related activities as required. Coordinates physical security administrative and operational matters with management, union officials, local law enforcement, and client/customers to ensure continuity of operations. Manages the activities and provides leadership direction to the professional, technical, and support staff within the organization unit.

Qualification guidelines

Bachelor's degree in an area of study relevant to this position and more than 6 years progressive experience in the armed forces security, military police, or with a major law enforcement, public, or private sector security organization. Must have a background, which would not preclude a security clearance granted.

Supervisor, physical security, unarmed

Job Code 443

Job description

Under general direction, supervises the personnel engaged in the physical security function for the organization. Assists in the development of an efficient and safe operation of the organization's physical security operations. Responsible for supervising and monitoring the systems associated with the flow of personnel and vehicular traffic entering and exiting organization's property. Develops and implements policies and procedures to audit personnel/visitor security clearances. Identifies and recommends electronic access control equipment designed to detect unauthorized entry into facilities or property. Develops procedures to prevent unauthorized entry into the organization's physical assets, and upon detection, supervises the personnel that isolates, negotiates, and/or escort individual(s) to a containment area. Assists in managing the loss prevention and detection services and enforces administrative procedures. Supervises the development and enhancement of security inspection procedures to prevent safety hazards, and to ensure the proper procedures are followed. Oversees the handling of emergency situations, including employee injuries. Monitors performance and assignments of personnel and makes periodic inspections to insure they are properly equipped, trained, and fulfilling their duties in compliance with organization's policies. Monitors and directs emergency response operational plans and related activities as required. Provides direct supervision to guard force, to include scheduling, coaching, staffing, and performance development.

Qualification guidelines

High school diploma or equivalent and more than 5 years progressive experience with a law enforcement, public, or private sector security organization. Knowledge of security systems and equipment in a business environment is necessary. Must have a background, which would not preclude a security clearance granted.

Security guard 3, unarmed

Job Code 447

Job description

Under general supervision performs assigned tasks from detailed instructions. Protects the organization's physical assets by maintaining and safeguarding the physical perimeter, exterior, and interior perimeters of the facility. Patrols, stands guard, and protects the facilities by foot and/or vehicle to detect or prevent illegal/unauthorized activities. Provides security protection for all organizational facilities, classified material and personnel within areas of responsibility to preclude unauthorized access, theft, or intentional destruction. Monitors the flow of personnel and vehicular traffic entering and exiting the building. Audits personnel/visitor security clearances and control activities to verify personal and organization ID. Maintains and updates visitor logs, commercial deliveries, and outside contractors entering and exiting the facility. Visually inspects common areas to prevent any hazards, and ensures proper safety procedures are followed. Monitors electronic perimeter control devises to detect any unauthorized entry into facility, and communicates any detection. Escort's guests and organization personnel throughout the facility as directed. Oversees the handling of emergency situations, including employee injuries. Prevents unauthorized entry into the company, and upon detection, isolates, negotiates, and escorts individual(s) to a containment area. Acts as a lead security guard to ensures safety of personnel by checking and monitoring of all equipment in guard areas. Maintains an in-depth knowledge of all security orders, written and oral, pertaining to assigned duties. Acts as a lead guard when required.

Qualification guidelines

High school diploma or equivalent and more than 3 years progressive experience with a law enforcement, public, or private sector security organization. Knowledge of security systems and equipment in a business environment is preferred. Must have a background, which would not preclude a security clearance granted.

Security guard 2, unarmed
Job Code 448

Job description

Under direct supervision performs assigned tasks from detailed instructions, established policies, and procedures. Protects the organizations physical assets by maintaining and safeguarding the physical perimeter, exterior, and interior perimeters of the facility. Patrols, stands guard, and protects the facilities by foot and/or vehicle to detect or prevent illegal/unauthorized activities. Provides security protection for all organizational facilities, classified material, and personnel within areas of responsibility to preclude unauthorized access, theft, or intentional destruction. Monitors the flow of personnel and vehicular traffic entering and exiting the building. Audits personnel/visitor security clearances and controls activities to verify personal and organization ID. Maintains and updates visitor logs, commercial deliveries, and outside contractors entering and exiting the facility. Visually inspects common areas to prevent any hazards, and ensures proper safety procedures are followed. Assists in the handling of emergency situations, including employee injuries. Prevents unauthorized entry into the company, and upon detection, isolates, negotiates, and escorts individual(s) to a containment area. Performs escort duties as appropriate. Maintains knowledge of all security orders, written and oral, pertaining to assigned duties.

Qualification guidelines

High school diploma or equivalent and more than 2 years progressive experience with a law enforcement, public, or private sector security organization. Knowledge of security systems and equipment in a business environment is preferred. Must have a background, which would not preclude a security clearance granted.

Security guard 1, unarmed

Job Code 449

Job description

Under immediate supervision performs routine, assigned tasks from detailed instructions, established policies, and procedures. Assists in the protection of the organizations physical assets by maintaining and safeguarding the physical facility, including the exterior and interior perimeters. Patrols, stands guard, and protects the facilities by foot and/or vehicle to detect or prevent illegal/unauthorized activities. Assists in providing security protection for all organizational facilities and personnel within areas of responsibility to preclude unauthorized access, theft, or intentional destruction. Assists in monitoring the flow of personnel and vehicular traffic entering and exiting the building. Logs personnel/visitor security clearances and controls activities to verify personal and company ID. Maintains and updates visitor logs, commercial deliveries, and outside contractors entering and exiting the facility. Visually inspects common areas to prevent any hazards, and notifies a senior guard when appropriate, to ensure proper safety procedures are followed. Prevents unauthorized entry into the company, and upon detection and with the assistance of a senior security guard, isolates, negotiates, and escorts individual(s) to a containment area. Performs escort duties as appropriate.

Qualification guidelines

High school diploma or equivalent and a minimum of 1 year experience with a law enforcement, public, or private sector security organization. Knowledge of security systems and equipment in a business environment is preferred. Must have a background, which would not preclude a security clearance granted.

Console operators
Job Code 450

Job description
Under direct supervision performs assigned tasks from detailed instructions, established policies, and procedures. Protects the organization's physical assets by maintaining and safeguarding the physical perimeter, exterior, and interior perimeters of the facility. Provides security protection by utilizing and monitoring the organization's building automation system, electronic surveillance systems, and other monitoring devices. Utilizes and maintains electronic surveillance and detection systems through security console operations to include security, fire, access control, heating, ventilation, and air conditioning (HVAC), and executive support. Based on console indications or event(s), identifies, initiates and coordinates appropriate response/notification based on security guidelines. Provides first point of contact for situations involving off-site facilities, medical services, computer center, weekend media inquires, and consumer hotline. Enters and retrieves data utilizing the organization's security management system. Assists in the smooth operation of post and shift operations. Keeps accurate log of events and occurrences based on security guidelines. Acts as an alternate lead security guard as required.

Qualification guidelines
High school diploma or equivalent required with 4 years progressive experience. Knowledge of security systems, devices, and building automation systems in a corporate environment preferred.

Top compliance and ethics executive (senior compliance/ethics officer—global)

Job Code 700

Job description

This position has global accountability for developing and directing the organization's compliance and ethics function for the total corporation worldwide, under executive management direction based on predetermined goal and objects. The incumbent in this position may also have responsibilities within other major functions: legal, human resources, auditing, etc. Determines appropriateness of corporate-wide compliance initiatives; provides leadership and oversight to ensure development and implementation of strategies, policies, and programs. Responsible for all activities relating to standards of conduct, to include ethical relationships with customers, contractors, suppliers, employees, shareholders, and other stakeholders. Provides leadership in the development of a compliance risk management program to assess, prioritize, and manage legal and regulatory compliance, facilitating the systematic assessment and management of compliance risks. Responsible for the company-wide confidential reporting program ("Helpline") allowing employees, customers, contractors, and other stakeholders to disclose violations of the corporation's ethical standards, violations of law, or corporate policy relating to such matters without fear of retaliation. Responsible for effectively managing the training, communications, and publications for the ethics and compliance policies, procedures, and practices to all employees and agents. Provides expert advice and interpretation of the company's code of conduct and policies and procedures. Accountable for conducting investigations into alleged violations of company ethics and business conduct and make recommendations for resolution of misconduct including penalties and other appropriate action based on severity of the case. May be accountable for ensuring compliance with U.S. Government procurement and contract compliance laws and regulations. Provides comprehensive reports to the top executive and various committees of the board of directors. Works closely with the cognizant staff functions, legal, finance, internal auditing, human resources, as well as, business unit senior management.

Qualification guidelines

JD or master's degree and more than 10 years work experience; or bachelor's degree and more than 15 years work experience. Minimum of 8 years of management responsibilities and 6 years relevant work in human resources, finance, internal auditing, legal, or security.

Corporate manager, compliance and ethics (domestic only)
Job Code 710

Job description

Plans, directs, and manages on a day-by-day basis the corporation's comprehensive compliance and ethics function under senior management direction based on predetermined goals and objectives. Participates in the development and implementation of strategies for all activities relating to the standards of conduct, and ethical relationships with customers, contractors, suppliers, employees, stakeholders, and the communities in which the organization operates. Provides direction in the development of a compliance risk management program to assess, prioritize, and manage legal and regulatory compliance risks. Responsible for effectively communicating the ethics, compliance, and business conduct standards and procedures to all employees and other agents. Provides expert advice and interpretation of the code of compliance and ethics, including the applicability of the organization's policies and programs. Works with other subject matter experts to develop the most appropriate methods for maintaining employee awareness of the program and pertinent laws or regulations pertaining to the organization's business. Responsible for preemptive/preventative studies, workforce analysis, monitoring the organizations compliance in responding to specialized areas of employment, employment opportunity/affirmative action and other business practices. Ensures there are consistency and completeness of internal, external, and governmental reporting while managing and coordinating documentation and monitoring efforts. May be responsible for managing the company-wide confidential reporting program ("Helpline") allowing employees, customers, contractors, and other stakeholders to disclose alleged violations of the corporation's ethical standards, violations of law, or corporate policy. Ensures that appropriate and timely responses are provided to inquiries. Monitors progress of investigations of alleged violations of the laws or regulations pertaining to the business, summarizes, documents, and maintains accurate records of issues handled. Works with various committees within the corporation that establish policy on a variety of procurement matters. Coordinates closely with the senior executive staff and internal auditing, finance, human resources and legal personnel relative to application, interpretation, and enforcement policies, and procedures. Provides leadership direction to the professional staff within the ethics and compliance function.

Qualification guidelines

Master's degree and more than 5 years experience in internal auditing, finance, human resources or legal functions; or a bachelor's degree and more than 8 years experience. Work experience should include a minimum of 5 years of management responsibility.

Manager, regulatory compliance

Job Code 720

Job description

Plans and directs the business compliance function for the total corporation under senior management direction based on predetermined goals and objectives. Provides corporate-wide focus for efforts relating to compliance with government procurement laws and regulations and with the organization's policies on business ethics and conduct in contracting with government agencies, including oversight responsibility for government contract compliance audit and training functions. Works with various functions within the corporation to establish policy on a variety of procurement matters, including government accounting, government property, and independent research and development issues. Provides guidance and expertise in the development and maintenance of the company's compliance risk management program to assess, prioritize, and manage legal and regulatory compliance risks based on benchmarking research, facilitating the systematic assessment, and management of compliance risks. Maintains an expertise on government procurement laws. Reviews corporate policies, systems, and procedures with respect to procurement matters and assists in drafting such policies to ensure that they establish a level of conduct that complies with applicable laws. Provides oversight and coordination for government contract training, policy, and related relationships within operating units and external organizations including suppliers. Conducts internal reviews to evaluate effectiveness of compliance efforts and to identify deficiencies in meeting the organization's expectations in its procurement practices. Interacts with government agencies in the conduct of investigations and audits on procurement/commercial matters. Position requires a thorough knowledge of the corporation's business strategies, policies, standards, and practices. Manages responsibilities within approved budget. In fulfilling these responsibilities, the incumbent must work closely with cognizant staff functions, including government contract compliance audit, internal audit, finance, legal, and human resources.

Qualification guidelines

JD or master's degree and more than 5 years experience; or bachelor's degree and more than 8 years experience. Work experience should include a minimum of 3 years of management responsibility and 5 years or more relevant work in domestic and international government regulatory compliance and laws.

Business unit manager, compliance and ethics
Job Code 735

Job description
Plans, directs, and manages on a day-by-day basis the corporation's comprehensive ethics and compliance function under the direction of senior management in an operating business unit based on predetermined goals and objectives. Participates in the development and implementation of strategies for all activities relating to the standards of conduct, and ethical relationships with customers, contractors, suppliers, employees, stakeholders, and the communities in which the organization operates. Responsible for effectively communicating the ethics and compliance standards and procedures to all employees and other agents, through training programs and publications. Provides expert advice and interpretation of the code of ethics and compliance, including the applicability of the organization's policies and programs to specific situations. Works with other subject matter experts to develop the most appropriate methods for maintaining employee awareness of the program and pertinent laws or regulations pertaining to the organization's business. May be responsible for managing the confidential reporting program ("Helpline") allowing employees, customers, contractors, and other stakeholders to disclose alleged violations of the corporation's ethical standards, violations of law, or corporate policy. Ensures that appropriate and timely responses are provided to inquiries. Monitors progress of investigations of alleged violations of the laws or regulations pertaining to the business, summarizes, documents, and maintains accurate records of issues handled. Provides direction in the development of a compliance risk management program to assess, prioritize, and manage legal and regulatory compliance risks. Works with various committees within the business unit that establishes policy on a variety of procurement matters. Coordinates with the business unit's senior executive, internal auditing, human resources, and legal personnel relative to application, interpretation, and enforcement of the corporation's policies and procedures. Manages responsibilities within approved budget. Provides leadership direction to the professional staff within the ethics and business conduct function.

Qualification guidelines
Master's degree and more than 3 years experience in internal auditing, finance, human resources, or legal; or bachelor's degree and more than 5 years experience. Work experience should include a minimum of 2 years of management responsibility and relevant work in government regulatory compliance and laws.

Senior compliance and ethics specialist

Job Code 740

Job description

Works under consultative direction toward predetermined goals and objectives. Assignments are usually self-initiated. Determines and pursues courses of action necessary to obtain desired results. Responsible for implementing and monitoring activities relating to standards of conduct, and ethical relationships with customers, contractors, suppliers, employees, stakeholders, and the communities in which the organization is conducting their business. Responsible for the overall implementation of action required to resolve work-related issues identified from various employee information gathering efforts. Provides analysis for management to make appropriate decisions in matters of complex and sensitive ethics and compliance matters related to the areas of employment and business practices. Provides expert advice and interpretation of the code of ethics and compliance, including the applicability of the organization's policies and programs to specific situations. Participates in the development and monitors the communication of the ethics and compliance standards and procedures to all employees and other agents, through training programs and publications. May participate in the implementation and maintenance of the company-wide confidential reporting systems ("Helpline") allowing all employees, customers, contractors, and other stakeholders to disclose violations of the corporation's ethical standards, violations of law, or corporate policy. May coordinate casework distribution within the corporate ethics and compliance function for the confidential reporting system and assures that the rules of confidentiality are rigorously observed and assures that appropriate and timely responses from the appropriate personnel are provided for inquiries. Advises supervisors and directs employees to the organization's dispute resolution processes. Coordinates with auditing, finance, human resources, and legal departments regarding the application, interpretation, and enforcement of the code of conduct and policies and procedures. Participates as an expert resource in the design and development of employee education and training programs. Must have thorough knowledge of the corporation's business strategies, policies, standards, and practices. May act as a lead person or technical expert on major ethics and compliance projects.

Qualification guidelines

Master's degree and more than 5 years experience in internal auditing, finance, human resources or legal functions; or bachelor's degree and more than 8 years experience in internal auditing, finance, human resources, or legal functions.

Compliance and ethics specialist
Job Code 745

Job description

Works under very general direction. Independently determines and develops approaches to solutions. Work is reviewed upon completion for adequacy in meeting objectives. Works on assignments to monitor activities relating to standards of conduct, and ethical relationships with customers, contractors, suppliers, employees, and the communities in which the organization is conducting their business. Assists with the overall implementation of action required to resolve work-related issues identified from various employee information gathering efforts. Provides analysis for management to make appropriate decisions in matters of sensitive ethics and compliance matters with all rules, policies, procedures, and codes of conduct related to areas of employment and business practices. Coordinates and participates with other subject matter experts on the corporation's risk management program to assess, prioritize, and manage legal and regulatory compliance risks. Participates in effectively communicating the ethics and compliance policies, procedures, and practices to all employees and other agents, through publications, training, and education programs. May provide analysis, advice, and consultation on employee issues as a vital constituent in business planning and major organization changes. May participate in the implementation and maintenance of the company-wide confidential reporting program ("Helpline") allowing all employees, customers, contractors, and other stakeholders to disclose violations of the corporation's ethical standards, violations of law, or corporate policy. Assures that appropriate and timely responses from the appropriate personnel are provided for inquiries. May coordinate casework distribution within the corporate ethics and compliance function for the confidential reporting program and assures that the rules of confidentiality are rigorously observed. Monitors progress of investigations, summarizes, documents, and maintains accurate records of issues handled. Coordinates closely with internal auditing, finance, human resources, and legal departments relative to application, interpretation, and enforcement of the code and the corporation's policies and procedures. Participates as an expert resource in the design and development of employee education and training programs regarding compliance with applicable laws, regulations, and code.

Qualification guidelines

Master's degree and more than 3 years experience in internal auditing, finance, human resources, or legal functions; or bachelor's degree and more than 6 years experience in internal auditing, finance, human resources, or legal functions.

Position Compensation Trends

5

Detailed results of a compensation survey on security jobs are beyond the scope of this book, but it behooves security professionals to at least have some idea of the compensation levels for various positions and how those levels have changed over time. Therefore, we are including generalized graphs to describe the overall salary trends for various positions (based on job descriptions in Chapter 4).

These trend graphs are derived from a compensation study conducted by the Foushée Group. It is important to note that the graphs are a snapshot in time over a period of years to show the value of a position to the market based on a set of position descriptions. The graphs can be helpful to any security leader or manager who is responsible for recommending the amounts of salaries or bonuses, as long as they are used intelligently and interpreted appropriately. We must always keep in mind that the graphs represent a broad-based view.

For many security professionals, these graphs may be their first exposure to this kind of information; many probably did not even know a security compensation study exists. At last, they now have some real numbers, based on real information, to support discussions of pay levels for security employees. Previously, human resource professionals may have had such information, but now the security professional can also participate in discussions about salary and bonus levels with some basis of quantitative knowledge. (See Chapter 3 for a discussion of compensation processes and how to get involved.)

It is interesting to note that the trend of wage and salary increases for security-related jobs has often been steeper in recent years than the national average for all jobs, driven by an increased importance of security since 9/11, and by the need for security professionals to expand their skill-sets. It is also notable that wages and salaries can vary based on the geographic location of a job (especially nonexempt jobs), the industry sector a job serves and other variables, the specifics of which are also beyond the scope of this book.

At the very least, the intent of providing wage and salary graphs is to encourage security managers and directors to become more proactively involved in discussions about salaries and bonuses. They should also encourage their human resource departments to participate in third-party wage and salary surveys in order to ensure the availability of usable information on compensation for security professionals, now and in the future.

The following charts show trends in total cash compensation paid (annual base wage and salary plus the annual cash bonus and/or cash incentive paid) for all employees that were matched to the position accountabilities and qualifications.

The data is not intended for compensation planning purposes, but rather as a graphic representation of historic market data for each position surveyed in the compensation report. Companies requiring specific data for compensation planning purposes should contact the Foushée Group, Inc. to discuss the annual Security and Compliance Compensation Survey.

Compensation trend charts

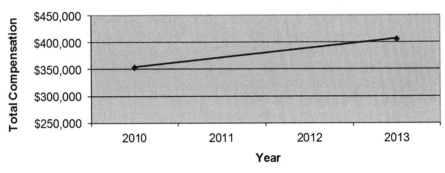

FIGURE 5.1

Compensation practice trend data: Top Global Security Executive (CSO) (Job Code 100).

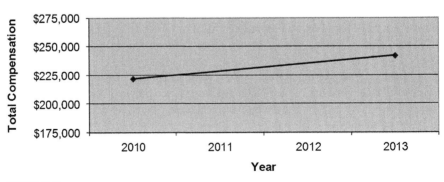

FIGURE 5.2

Compensation practice trend data: Second Level Global Security Executive (Job Code 101).

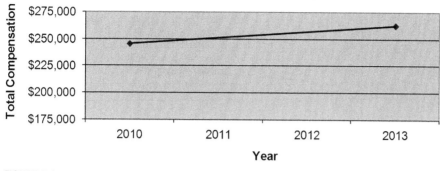

FIGURE 5.3

Compensation practice trend data: Top Security Executive, International (Job Code 200).

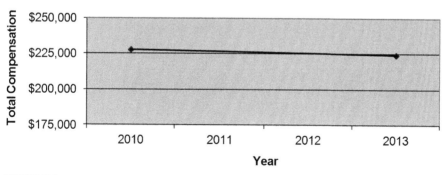

FIGURE 5.4

Compensation practice trend data: Senior Regional Manager, International Security (Job Code 210).

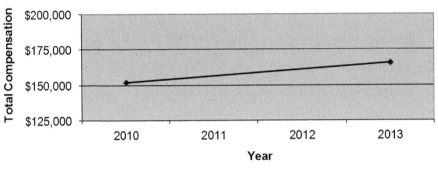

FIGURE 5.5

Compensation practice trend data: Regional Manager, International Security (Job Code 220).

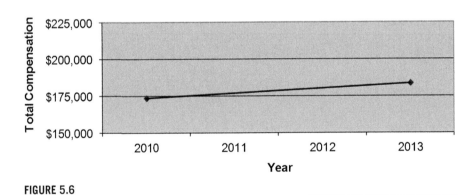

FIGURE 5.6

Compensation practice trend data: Manager, International Investigation (Job Code 225).

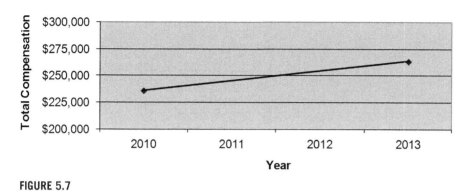

FIGURE 5.7

Compensation practice trend data: Top Security Executive, Domestic (Job Code 300).

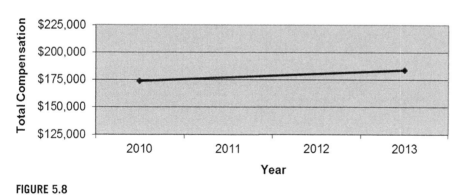

FIGURE 5.8

Compensation practice trend data: Senior Manager, Threat Analysis (Job Code 303).

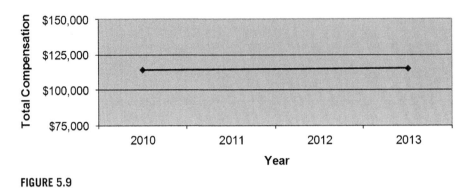

FIGURE 5.9

Compensation practice trend data: Senior Threat Analyst IV (Job Code 306).

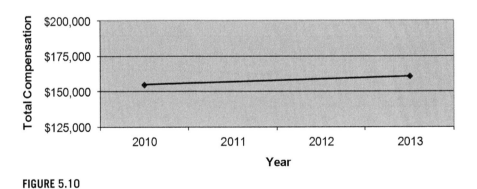

FIGURE 5.10

Compensation practice trend data: Senior Manager, Protective Services (HQ) (Job Code 310).

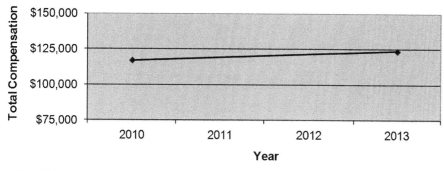

FIGURE 5.11

Compensation practice trend data: Senior Protective Services Agent IV (Job Code 314).

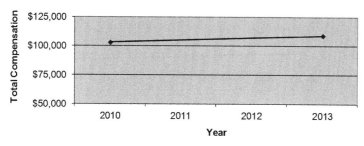

FIGURE 5.12

Compensation practice trend data: Protective Services Agent III (Job Code 315).

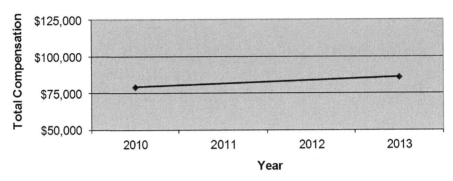

FIGURE 5.13

Compensation practice trend data: Protective Services Agent II (Job Code 316).

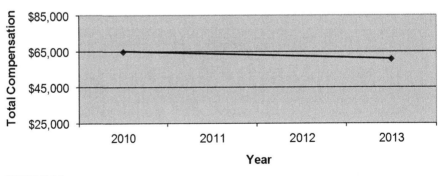

FIGURE 5.14

Compensation practice trend data: Protective Services Agent I (Job Code 317).

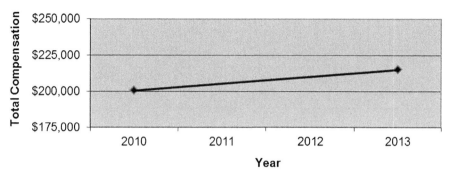

FIGURE 5.15

Compensation practice trend data: Director, Computer, Network and Information Security (Job Code 319).

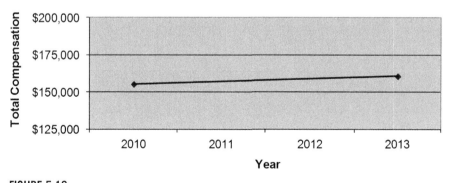

FIGURE 5.16

Compensation practice trend data: Manager, Computer and Information Security (Job Code 320).

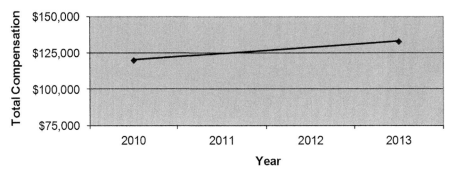

FIGURE 5.17

Compensation practice trend data: Senior Computer and Information Security Specialist IV (Job Code 321).

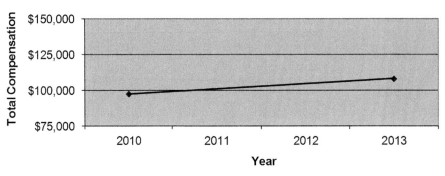

FIGURE 5.18

Compensation practice trend data: Computer and Information Security Specialist III (Job Code 322).

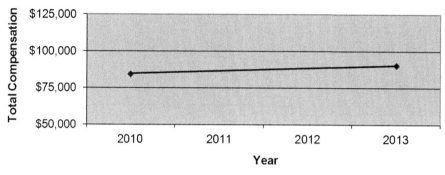

FIGURE 5.19

Compensation practice trend data: Computer and Information Security Specialist II (Job Code 323).

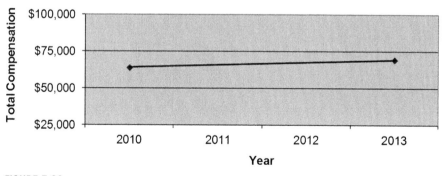

FIGURE 5.20

Compensation practice trend data: Computer and Information Security Specialist I (Job Code 324).

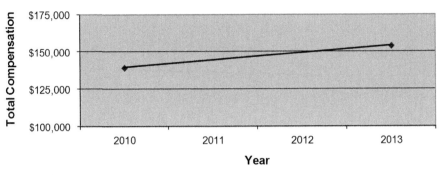

FIGURE 5.21

Compensation practice trend data: Manager, Network Security (Job Code 325).

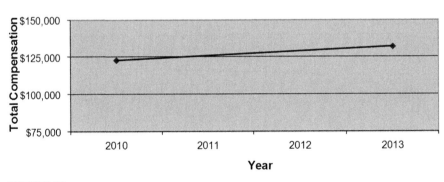

FIGURE 5.22

Compensation practice trend data: Senior Network Security Specialist IV (Job Code 326).

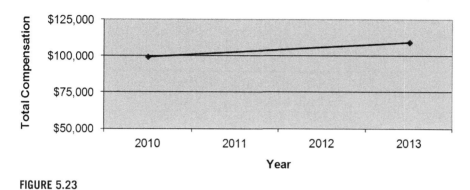

FIGURE 5.23

Compensation practice trend data: Network Security Specialist III (Job Code 327).

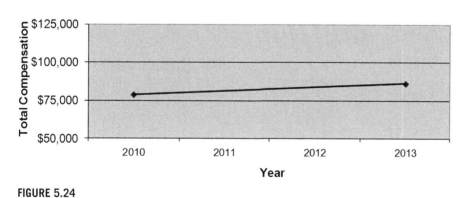

FIGURE 5.24

Compensation practice trend data: Network Security Specialist II (Job Code 328).

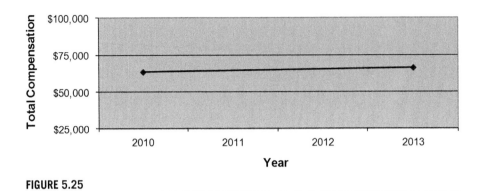

FIGURE 5.25

Compensation practice trend data: Network Security Specialist I (Job Code 329).

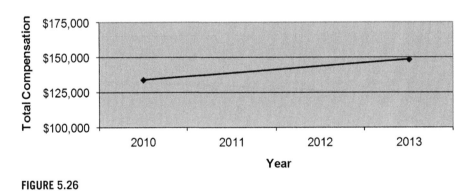

FIGURE 5.26

Compensation practice trend data: Manager, Domestic Investigation (Job Code 330).

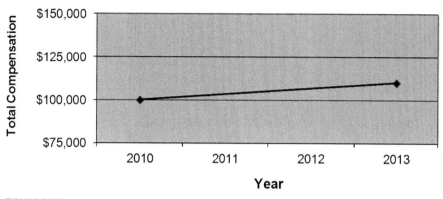

FIGURE 5.27

Compensation practice trend data: Supervisor, Domestic Investigation (Job Code 331).

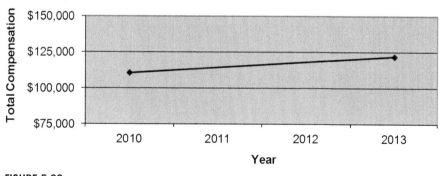

FIGURE 5.28

Compensation practice trend data: Senior Investigator IV (Job Code 334).

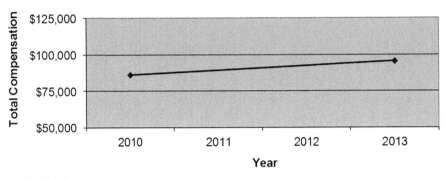

FIGURE 5.29

Compensation practice trend data: Investigator III (Job Code 335).

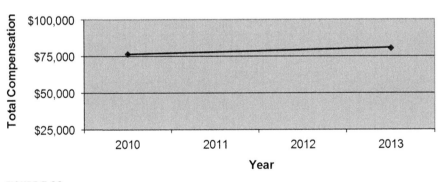

FIGURE 5.30

Compensation practice trend data: Investigator II (Job Code 336).

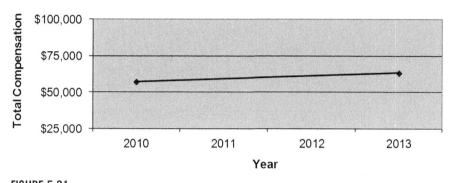

FIGURE 5.31

Compensation practice trend data: Investigator I (Job Code 337).

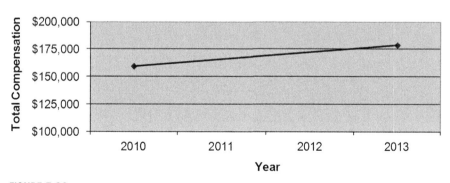

FIGURE 5.32

Compensation practice trend data: Senior Regional Manager, Domestic Security (Job Code 340).

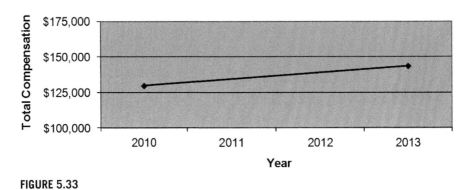

FIGURE 5.33

Compensation practice trend data: Regional Manager, Domestic Security (Job Code 341).

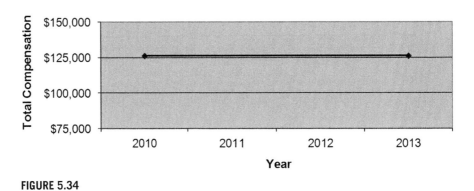

FIGURE 5.34

Compensation practice trend data: Manager, Business Unit Security (Job Code 342).

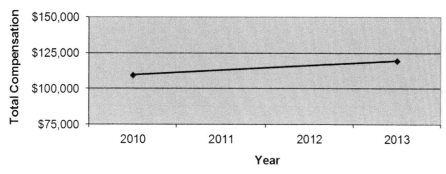

FIGURE 5.35

Compensation practice trend data: Senior Business Unit Security Manager IV (Job Code 344).

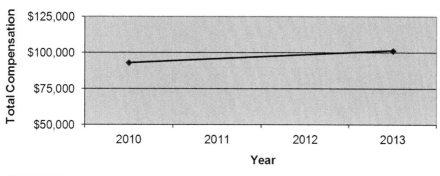

FIGURE 5.36

Compensation practice trend data: Business Unit Security Manager III (Job Code 345).

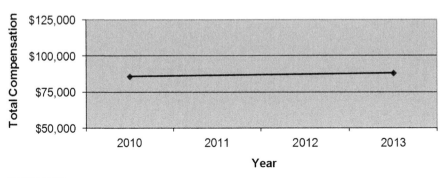

FIGURE 5.37

Compensation practice trend data: Business Unit Security Manager II (Job Code 346).

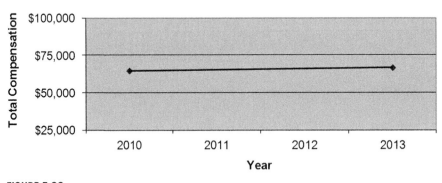

FIGURE 5.38

Compensation practice trend data: Business Unit Security Manager I (Job Code 347).

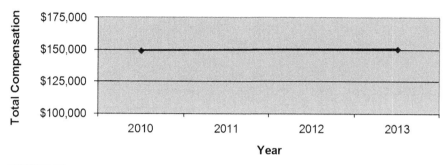

FIGURE 5.39

Compensation practice trend data: Manager, Emergency Preparedness/Disaster Recovery (Job Code 352).

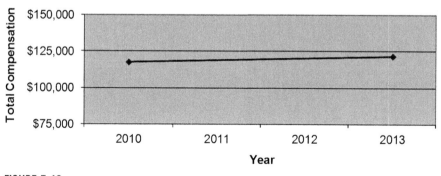

FIGURE 5.40

Compensation practice trend data: Senior Emergency Preparedness Specialist IV (Job Code 354).

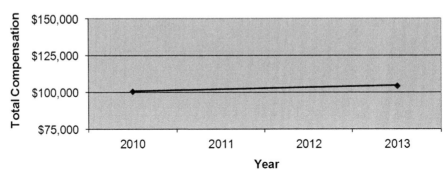

FIGURE 5.41

Compensation practice trend data: Emergency Preparedness Specialist III (Job Code 355).

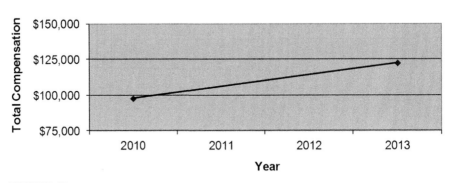

FIGURE 5.42

Compensation practice trend data: Senior Nuclear Accountability Specialist IV (Job Code 364).

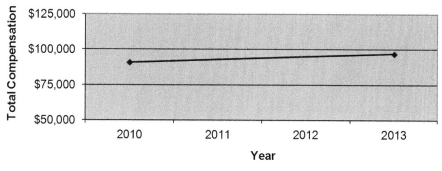

FIGURE 5.43

Compensation practice trend data: Nuclear Accountability Specialist III (Job Code 365).

Senior Manager, Product Protection Security (Job Code 368).
No data to compare.

Manager, Product Protection Security (Job Code 369).
No data to compare.

Senior Product Protection Security Specialist IV (Job Code 370).
No data to compare.

Product Protection Security Specialist III (Job Code 371).
No data to compare.

Product Protection Security Specialist II (Job Code 372).
No data to compare.

Product Protection Security Specialist I (Job Code 373).
No data to compare.

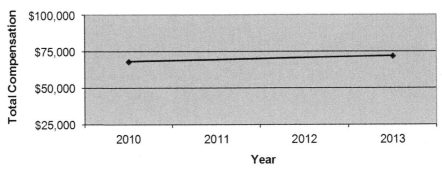

FIGURE 5.44

Compensation practice trend data: Security Clearance Specialist II (Job Code 386).

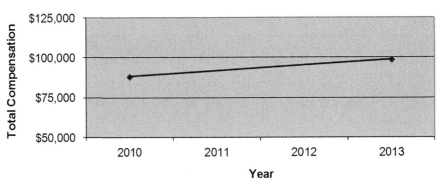

FIGURE 5.45

Compensation practice trend data: Physical Security Systems Specialist III (Job Code 392).

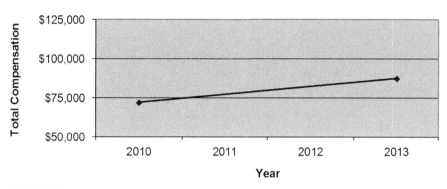

FIGURE 5.46

Compensation practice trend data: Physical Security Systems Specialist II (Job Code 393).

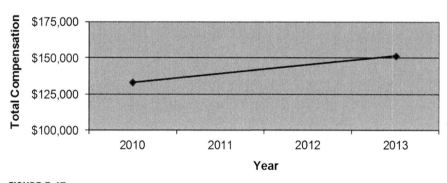

FIGURE 5.47

Compensation practice trend data: Senior Manager, Product Protection Programs (Job Code 401).

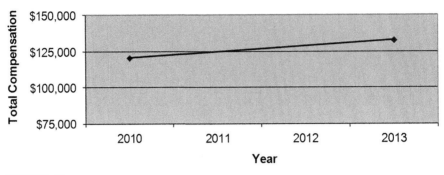

FIGURE 5.48

Compensation practice trend data: Manager, Corporate Security Programs (Job Code 402).

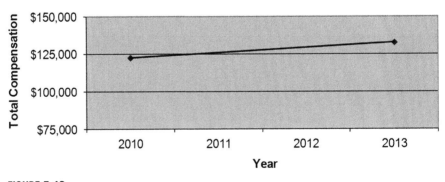

FIGURE 5.49

Compensation practice trend data: Manager, Security Systems and Training (Job Code 412).

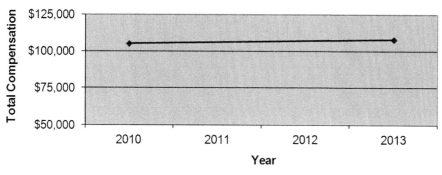

FIGURE 5.50

Compensation practice trend data: Senior Security Training and Awareness Specialist IV (Job Code 414).

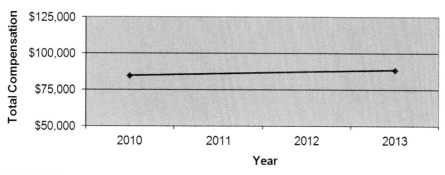

FIGURE 5.51

Compensation practice trend data: Security Training and Awareness Specialist III (Job Code 415).

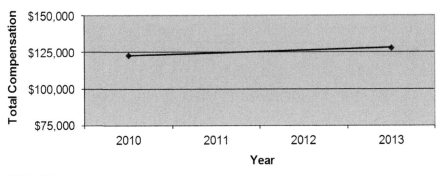

FIGURE 5.52

Compensation practice trend data: Manager, Classified Security Projects (Job Code 422).

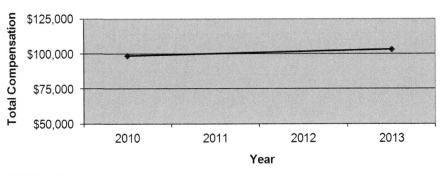

FIGURE 5.53

Compensation practice trend data: Senior Classified Security Specialist IV (Job Code 424).

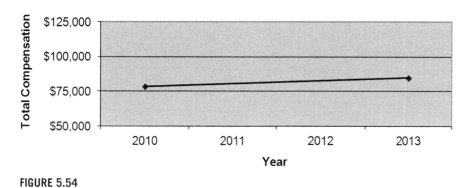

FIGURE 5.54

Compensation practice trend data: Classified Security Specialist III (Job Code 425).

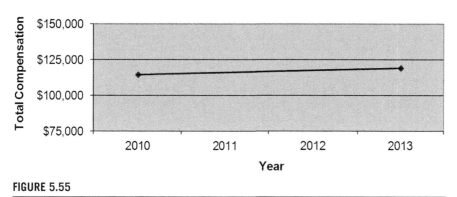

FIGURE 5.55

Compensation practice trend data: Manager, Protective Forces, Armed (Job Code 432).

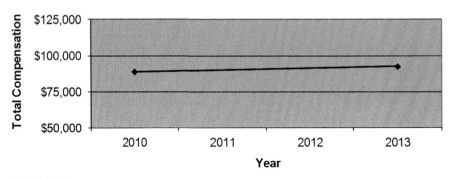

FIGURE 5.56

Compensation practice trend data: Officer in Charge, Protective Forces, Armed (Job Code 433).

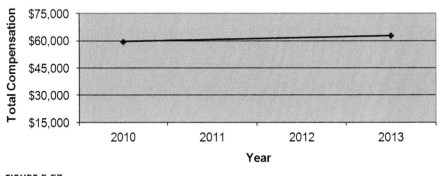

FIGURE 5.57

Compensation practice trend data: Security Officer 3, Armed (Job Code 437).

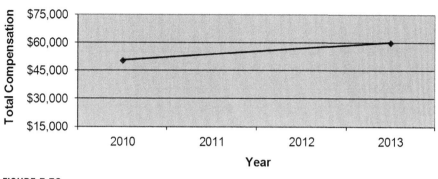

FIGURE 5.58

Compensation practice trend data: Security Officer 2, Armed (Job Code 438).

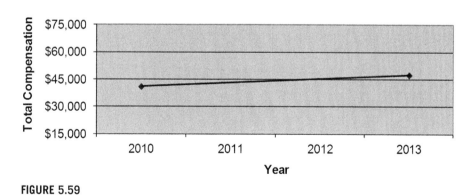

FIGURE 5.59

Compensation practice trend data: Security Officer 1, Armed (Job Code 439).

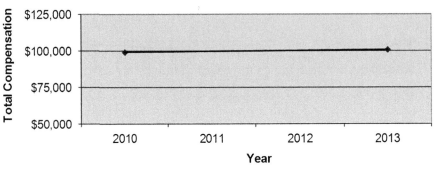

FIGURE 5.60

Compensation practice trend data: Manager, Physical Security, Unarmed (Job Code 442).

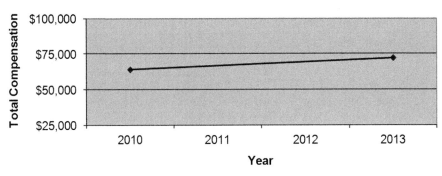

FIGURE 5.61

Compensation practice trend data: Supervisor, Physical Security, Unarmed (Job Code 443).

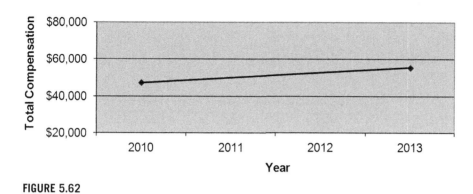

FIGURE 5.62

Compensation practice trend data: Security Officer 3, Unarmed (Job Code 447).

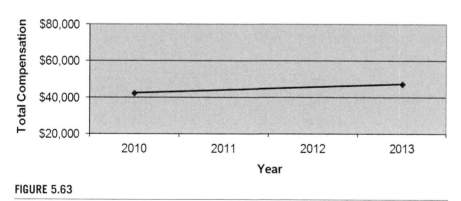

FIGURE 5.63

Compensation practice trend data: Security Officer 2, Unarmed (Job Code 448).

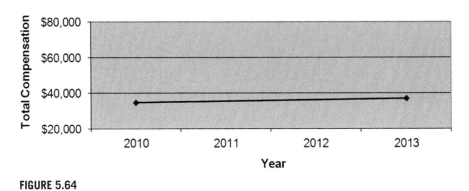

FIGURE 5.64

Compensation practice trend data: Security Officer 1, Unarmed (Job Code 449).

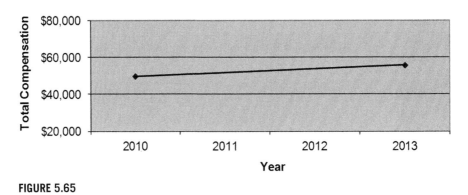

FIGURE 5.65

Compensation practice trend data: Console Operator (Job Code 450).

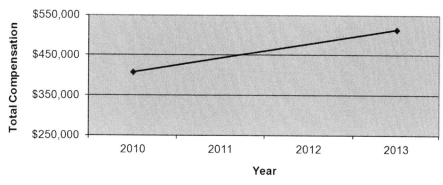

FIGURE 5.66

Compensation practice trend data: Top Compliance and Ethics Executive (Job Code 700).

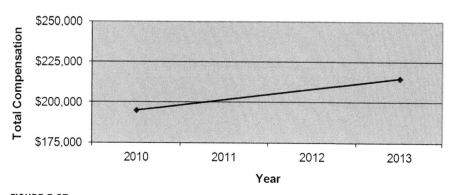

FIGURE 5.67

Compensation practice trend data: Corporate Manager, Compliance and Ethics (Job Code 710).

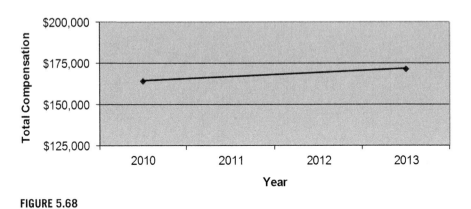

FIGURE 5.68

Compensation practice trend data: Manager, Regulatory Compliance (Job Code 720).

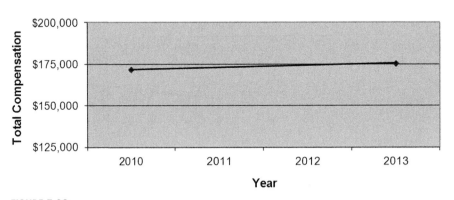

FIGURE 5.69

Compensation practice trend data: Business Unit Manager, Compliance and Ethics (Job Code 735).

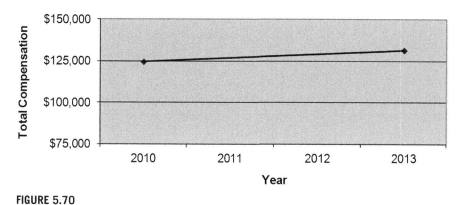

FIGURE 5.70

Compensation practice trend data: Senior Compliance and Ethics Specialist (Job Code 740).

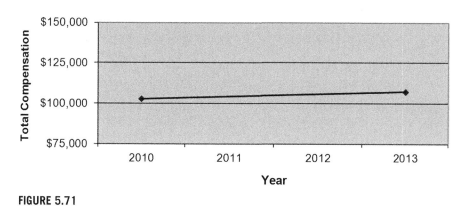

FIGURE 5.71

Compensation practice trend data: Compliance and Ethics Specialist (Job Code 745).

Career Resources

6

This chapter includes a compilation of resources related to security careers, including certifications, membership organizations, publications, and job listing sites. It is designed to provide a single reference point for anyone looking for a new security job or change in direction, or anyone surveying his or her options for beginning a career in security.

It is important to note that although certifications can be valuable, especially at the beginning of a security career, they are often a narrow measure of operational knowledge, and their relevance tends to decrease as careers transition to middle or senior management.

Please also note that the descriptions of the resources listed in this chapter come directly from the Web site of the respective organization. We encourage you to visit the Web sites and/or contact the organizations directly for more information about membership, training, and courses offered. This list is for informational purposes only; no listing included here should be construed as an endorsement of any kind by the authors or the Security Executive Council. It is impossible for any brief listing to be totally comprehensive, and clearly new resources emerge over time.

Associations
Alliance for Enterprise Security Risk Management

76552 Begonia Lane
Palm Desert, CA 92211
Telephone: 760-518-0425
Web site: http://www.qualified-audit-partners.be/index.php?cont=817&lgn=3
Area of expertise/focus: Qualified advanced partners' business is to assess, govern, and guide transformation in the finance, energy, high technology, health care, service, and public sectors.
Training: Audit, global risk and control, custom.

The Alliance for Enterprise Security Risk Management (AESRM) was formed by three leading international security associations: ASIS International, International Systems Audit and Control Association (ISACA), and the Information Systems Security Association (ISSA). The alliance brings together more than 90,000 global security professionals with broad security backgrounds and skills to address the significant increase and complexity of security-related risks to international commerce from terrorism, cyberattacks, Internet viruses, theft, fraud, extortion, and other threats.

American Board of Forensic Document Examiners

7887 San Felipe, Suite 122
Houston, TX 77063
Telephone: 713-784-9537
Web site: http://www.abfde.org/
Membership/registration/certification/cost: Certification
Area of expertise/focus: Forensic document examination
The American Board of Forensic Document Examiners, Inc.® (ABFDE) was established in 1977. The Board's objectives are twofold: to establish, maintain, and enhance standards of qualification for those who practice forensic document examination, and to certify applicants who comply with ABFDE requirements for this expertise. In doing so, the Board aims to safeguard the public interest by ensuring that anyone who claims to be a specialist in forensic document examination does, in fact, possess the necessary skills and qualifications.

American College of Forensic Examiners Institute

2750 E. Sunshine Street
Springfield, MO 65804
Telephone: 800-423-9737
Web site: http://www.acfei.com/about_acfei/
Area of expertise/focus: Forensic examination
Social media: Twitter: @ACFEI; Facebook
Membership: $65–$165/annually
Certification: The American College of Forensic Examiners Institute (ACFEI) has elevated standards through education, credentials, basic, and advanced training as well as diplomate and fellow status. It offers nine different forensic certification programs.
   Training: Courses are also offered online to provide applicants the choice of studying at their own pace. A few of the online programs offered are the certified forensic accountant (Cr.FA); certificate in homeland security (CHS); and the sensitive security information, certified® program.
   ACFEI is an independent, scientific, and professional association representing forensic examiners worldwide. ACFEI actively promotes the dissemination of forensic information and the continued advancement of forensic examination and consultation across the many professional fields of membership.

American Fuel & Petrochemical Manufacturers

1667 K Street, NW, Suite 700
Washington, DC 20006
Telephone: 202-457-0480
Web site: http://www.afpm.org/
Area of expertise/focus: Fuel trade association

Membership: Associate and regular
Social media: Facebook
The National Petrochemical & Refiners Association changed its name to the American Fuel & Petrochemical Manufacturers (AFPM). AFPM members serve you and America by manufacturing vital products for your life every day, while strengthening America's economic and national security.

American Polygraph Association

PO Box 8037
Chattanooga, TN 37414-0037
Telephone: 1-800-APA-8037
Web site: http://www.polygraph.org/
Area of expertise/focus: Polygraph organization
Social media: Facebook
Membership: $170
Established in 1966, the American Polygraph Association (APA) consists of over 2500 members dedicated to providing a valid and reliable means to verify the truth and establish the highest standards of moral, ethical, and professional conduct in the polygraph field. The APA continues to be a leading polygraph professional association, establishing standards of ethical practices, techniques, instrumentation, research, and advanced training and continuing educational programs.

American Society of Questioned Document Examiners

PO Box 18298
Long Beach, CA 90807
Telephone: 562-253-2589
Web site: http://www.asqde.org/contact/contact.html
Area of expertise/focus: Questioned document examination
Social media: Facebook
The objectives and purposes of the Society and of its members are to foster education, sponsor scientific research, establish standards, exchange experiences, and provide instruction in the field of questioned document examination, and to promote justice in matters that involve questions about documents.

Armed Forces Communications and Electronics Association

4400 Fair Lakes Court
Fairfax, VA 22033
Telephone: 800-336-4583
Web site: http://www.afcea.org/
Area of expertise/focus: Ethical information exchange
Social media: Twitter: @AFCEA; Facebook

Armed Forces Communications and Electronics Association (AFCEA) is an international organization that serves its members by providing a forum for the ethical exchange of information. AFCEA is dedicated to increasing knowledge through the exploration of issues relevant to its members in information technology, communications, and electronics for the defense, homeland security, and intelligence communities.

Asian Professional Security Association

901, Pragati Tower, 26, Rajendra Place
New Delhi-110 008, India
Telephone: 603-7806-4089
Web site: http://www.apsa-india.org/
Areas of expertise/focus: Electronic security systems, physical security, cash management
Social media: Facebook
Membership:$50–$500 annually
The Asian Professional Security Association (APSA) is a nonprofit, international organization of information security professionals and practitioners. It provides educational forums, publications, and peer interaction opportunities that enhance the knowledge, skill, and professional growth of its members.

Association of Certified Forensic Investigators of Canada

4 Iris Street
Huntsville, ON
P1H 1L8
Telephone: 416-226-3018
Web site: http://www.acfi.ca/
Area of expertise/focus: Forensic investigations
Social media: Facebook
Membership: Regular $100 and associate $245
Certification: Certified forensic investigator
The Association of Certified Forensic Investigators (Association) is a nonprofit Canadian organization whose objective is to promote and foster a national forum and governing body for the affiliation of professionals who provide to the public, governments, and employers, their expertise and services in the areas of fraud prevention, detection, and investigation.

Association of Certified Fraud Examiners

The Gregor Building
716 West Avenue
Austin, TX 78701

Telephone: 800-245-3321 (USA and Canada only)
Web site: http://www.cfenet.com/
Area of expertise/focus: Antifraud
Social media: Twitter: @TheACFE; Facebook
Certification: Certified fraud examiner
The Association of Certified Fraud Examiners (ACFE) is the world's largest antifraud organization and premier provider of antifraud training and education. Together with more than 65,000 members, the ACFE is reducing business fraud worldwide and inspiring public confidence in the integrity and objectivity within the profession.

Association of Certified Fraud Specialists

PO Box 348777
Sacramento, CA 95813
Telephone: 866-HEY-ACFS
Web site: http://www.acfsnet.org/
Area of expertise/focus: Antifraud
Social media: Twitter: @ACFSnet; Facebook
An educational, nonprofit headquartered in Sacramento, California, the Association of Certified Fraud Specialists (ACFS), provides low-cost learning and networking opportunities to law enforcement and public and private sector investigators, auditors, and other risk management professionals. The 501(c)(3) organization also administers the certified fraud specialist designation helping members who work in the antifraud profession achieve leadership status, attain higher levels of recognition, authenticate skills, and transform knowledge into a meaningful career.

Association of Former Intelligence Officers

AFIO Central Office
7700 Leesburg Pike, Ste 324
Falls Church, VA 22043
Telephone: 703 790 0320
Web site: http://www.afio.com/
Area of expertise/focus: Intelligence, counterterrorism, homeland security
Membership: Counterintelligence professional $60 to Nathan Hale fellow $1000
Social media: Twitter: @AFIO; Facebook
The Association of Former Intelligence Officers was incorporated in 1975 as a 501(c) 3 nonprofit, nonpolitical, educational association for current and former intelligence professionals and supporters of the U.S. intelligence community. The Association is based in the Commonwealth of Virginia.

Asia Crisis & Security Group

Hong Kong (SAR), China
Web site: http://www.acsgroup.org/
Area of expertise/focus: Crisis management
Membership: Membership is obtained through an introduction from a current Asia Crisis & Security Group member and submission of the entry criteria outlined on the membership page.

The group is comprised of security, crisis, and continuity professionals who are engaged in relevant in-house management roles for MNCs and NGOs. A small number of government employees are granted membership based on interaction with the industry in the Asia region.

Asian Professional Security Association

Chapters: Hong Kong, Bangkok, India, Malaysia, Singapore
Telephone:+852-2326-6366
Web sites: http://www.apsathailand.com/; http://www.aspa-india.org/; http://www.aspahk.org/; http://www.aspa-malaysia.com
Areas of expertise/focus: Electronic security systems, physical security, cash management
Membership: $50–500 annually
Social media: Facebook

Asian Professional Security Association was officially founded in Bangkok, Thailand in March 1994 following the successful holding of the 1st Asian International Security Conference. APSA–HK Chapter, being the first regional Chapter, was officially founded on 9th December, 1994. APSA–HK Chapter engages in promoting professional security within the security industry in Hong Kong. The APSA® is a nonprofit, international organization of information security professionals and practitioners. It provides educational forums, publications, and peer interaction opportunities that enhance the knowledge, skill, and professional growth of its members.

ASIS International

1625 Prince Street
Alexandria, VA 22314
Telephone: 703-519-6200
Web site: http://www.asisonline.org/
Membership: Regular $150; student $25
Certifications: Certified protection professional (CPP), professional certified investigator (PCI), physical security professional (PSP)
Area of expertise/focus: Asset protection
Social media: Twitter: @ASIS_Intl; Facebook; LinkedIn

ASIS International is a global community of 38,000 security practitioners, each of them has a role in the protection of assets—people, property, and/or information.

Australian Security Industry Association Limited

PO Box 1338
Crows Nest NWS 1585
Telephone: (02) 8425 4300
Web site: http://www.asial.com.au/
Area of expertise/focus: Private security industry
Membership: Corporate and provisional; associate

The Australian Security Industry Association Limited is the industry body for the Australian private security industry, dedicated to supporting members, promoting standards, and safeguarding public interests.

Canadian Security Association

50 Acadia Avenue, Suite 201
Markham, ON
L3R 0B3
Telephone: 905-513-0622
Web site: http://www.canasa.org/
Area of expertise/focus: Industry association
Membership: $46–$715
Training: Management, technical, sales programs, and courses offered
Social media: Twitter: @CANASA_News; Facebook; LinkedIn

Established in 1977, the Canadian Security Association (CANASA) is a national not-for-profit organization dedicated to advancing the security industry and supporting security professionals in Canada. CANASA protects and promotes the interests of its members and the safety of all Canadians through education, advocacy, and leadership.

The Canadian Council of Security Professionals

(formerly Canadian Society for Industrial Security)
PO Box 57006
Jackson Station
2 King Street West
Hamilton, ON
L8P 4W9
Telephone: 905-853-6523
Web site: http://www.csis-scsi.org/
Area of expertise/focus: Industry association

The Canadian Council of Security Professionals is undergoing a renewal and revitalization with the goal being to raise our profile, ensuring that those working in the industry in Canada, are ethical and using effective and efficient processes as well as maintaining a level of professionalism that will stand up to any scrutiny and set of standards both national and international.

Communications Fraud Control Association

4 Becker Farm Road, 4th Floor
PO Box 954
Roseland, NJ 07068
Telephone: 973-871-4032
Web site: http://www.cfca.org/
Area of expertise/focus: Fraud protection
Membership: Corporate, law enforcement, retired
Training: Educational events offered
Social media: LinkedIn
CFCA is an international association for revenue assurance, loss prevention, and fraud control through education and information.

Diplomatic Security Special Agents Association

PO Box 228
Dunn Loring, VA 22027
Telephone: 703-204-6127
Web site: http://www.dssaa.org/
Area of expertise/focus: Federal law enforcement
Membership: Membership for active, retired, or former Diplomatic Security (DS) special agents, and all who are currently associated with DS in some employment capacity (SEO, courier, support staff, contractors, etc.)
Social media: Facebook
DSSAA is not a government agency, but is a fraternal, benevolent association, classified as a non-profit 501(c)(6). The association exists to foster the development of professional and personal relationships between Diplomatic Security Service (DSS) Special Agents, DSS personnel (former and current), other fraternal law enforcement organizations (i.e., FOP), law enforcement agencies and members of the intelligence community. The DSSAA strives to establish a focal point of communication and promote the exchange of information regarding matters that are of mutual concern to DSSAA members.

While the DSSAA cannot serve as a bargaining unit, it endeavors to actively promote projects designed to support and benefit its members. Additionally, the DSSAA takes into account that an agent's family is an integral part of the DS organization. With agents being asked more and more to operate in hostile environments, the fact that the DSSAA is standing by to assist family members during a crisis offers some relief and support to the DS Agent serving overseas.

DRI International, Inc.

1115 Broadway, 12th Floor
New York, NY 10010
Web site: http://www.drii.org/
Area of expertise/focus: Disaster recovery
Social media: LinkedIn

DRI International was founded in 1988 as the Disaster Recovery Institute in order to develop a base of knowledge in contingency planning and the management of risk, a rapidly growing profession. DRI International administers educational and certification programs for those engaged in the practice of business continuity planning and management.

Energy Security Council

2711 FM 1960 West, Suite F-121
Houston, TX 77068
Telephone: 281-587-2700
Web site: http://www.energcysecuritycouncil.org
Area of expertise/focus: Energy sector security

The Energy Security Council, Inc. seeks to be recognized as the premiere energy sector security organization, adding value to the membership through education, information-sharing, networking, and sharing best security practices in order to enhance security within the sector.

European Corporate Security Association

Domain de Latour de Freins
Rue Engeland straat 555
B-1180 Brussels, Belgium
Telephone:+32 2 600 50 09
Web site: http://ecsa-eu.org/
Area of expertise/focus: EU corporate security
Membership: Individual $270; corporate $1050; industry $2100–$5200
Social media: Facebook; LinkedIn

The European Corporate Security Association (ECSA) is an association of professionals from the public, private, and academic sector who are active in, or contribute to the security, the continuity or the resilience of corporations, organizations and institutions. ECSA provides its members with a trusted forum for sharing of common issues & experiences; information and education; networking with comembers and third parties.

The European Institute

1001 Connecticut Avenue, NW, Suite 220
Washington, DC 20036
Telephone: 202-895-1670
Web site: www.europeaninstitute.org
Area of expertise/focus: Public and private sector security
Social media: Facebook; LinkedIn

As a leading Washington-based public-policy organization devoted solely to transatlantic affairs, The European Institute provides an independent forum in which key decision makers from both the public and private sectors in Europe and the United States can meet to discuss issues of common concern and develop effective and mutually beneficial solutions.

Federal Law Enforcement Officers Association

PO Box 326
Lewisberry, PA 17339
Telephone: 202-870-5503
Web site: http://www.fleoa.org/
Area of expertise/focus: Legal representation for federal law enforcement
Federal Law Enforcement Officers Association (FLEOA)® provides a legislative voice for the federal law enforcement community, and is frequently called upon to provide testimony at congressional hearings. FLEOA® monitors legislative issues that may impact federal law enforcement officers, and encourages its membership to contact their elected officials to express their concerns.

Federal Information Systems Security Educators' Association

100 Bureau Drive, Stop 8930
Gaithersburg, MD 20899-8930
Telephone: 301-975-2489
Web site: http://csrc.nist.gov/
Area of expertise/focus: Information security
Training: Federal Information Systems Security Educators' Association (FIS-SEA) conducts an annual fee-based conference and free workshops during the year
Social media: LinkedIn
The Federal Information Systems Security Educators' Association (FISSEA), founded in 1987, is an organization run by and for information systems security professionals to assist federal agencies in meeting their information systems security awareness, training, education, and certification responsibilities. FISSEA became a National Institute of Standards and Technology (NIST) program under the National Initiative for Cybersecurity Education in March 2011.

Fraud Women's Network

PO Box 60454
London E8 9A
Telephone:+44 (0) 7534 494779
Web site: http://www.fraudwomensnetwork.com/
Area of expertise/focus: Fraud prevention
Social media: LinkedIn
The Fraud Women's Network brings together women involved in all aspects of fraud prevention, detection, investigation, and prosecution.

High Technology Crime Investigation Association

3288 Goldstone Drive
Roseville, CA 95747
Telephone: 916-408-1751
Web site: http://www.htcia.org/

Area of expertise/focus: High tech crimes
Membership: $75
Training: Classes and labs offered
Social media: Facebook; LinkedIn

The High Technology Crime Investigation Association (HTCIA) was formed to provide education and collaboration to global members for the prevention and investigation of high tech crimes.

Illinois Security Chief's Association

PO Box 388085
Chicago, IL 60638
Telephone: 773-582-5252
Web site: http://www.securitychiefs.org/
Area of expertise/focus: Public and private law enforcement
Membership: $75
Training: Annual conferences; U.S. and Latin America training
Social media: LinkedIn

The Illinois Security Chief's Association (ISCA) has been the leading organization promoting cooperation between law enforcement and private security organizations. Throughout the years, ISCA have fostered collaborations with the FBI, U.S. Secret Service, Department of Homeland Security, Illinois State Police, Chicago Police Department, Chicago Fire Department, and other first responders throughout Illinois.

International Anti-Counterfeiting Coalition

1730 M Street NW
Suite 1020
Washington, DC 20036
Telephone: 202-223-6667
Web site: http://www.iacc.org
Area of expertise/focus: Intellectual property protection
Membership: $150 (Government officials) to $8000 (Law firms, IP owners, trade associations)
Training: Annual conferences; U.S. and Latin America training
Social media: LinkedIn

The International Anti-Counterfeiting Coalition's (IACC's) mission is to combat counterfeiting and piracy by promoting laws, regulations, and directives designed to render the theft of intellectual property undesirable and unprofitable. The IACC serves as an umbrella organization, offering anticounterfeiting programs designed to increase protection for patents, trademarks, copyrights, service marks, trade dress, and trade secrets.

International Association of Airport and Seaport Police

Web site: http://www.interportpolice.org
Area of expertise/focus: Data management (1PASS), information sharing (SRMX), training, learning exchanges (Plan "C"), international and domestic policy (IMO)

Social media: Twitter: @interportpolice; Facebook; MetroWatch

The InterPortPolice is an agency nonprofit organization working with law enforcement and public safety command leadership for over 43 years. If your jurisdiction or organization has responsibility over an airport, seaport, border, cruise, supply chain, or public transportation, you are encouraged to participate.

International Association of Privacy Professionals

75 Rochester Ave., Suite 4
Portsmouth, NH 03801
Telephone: 603-427-9200
Web site: http://www.privacyassociation.org/
Area of expertise/focus: Data management and protection
Membership: Individual; corporate; government; and not-for-profit groups
Social media: Facebook

The International Association of Privacy Professionals (IAPP) is the largest and most comprehensive global information privacy community and resource, helping practitioners develop and advance their careers and organizations manage and protect their data. More than just a professional association, the IAPP provides a home for privacy professionals around the world to gather, share experiences and enrich their knowledge.

International Association of Professional Security Consultants

575 Market St., Suite 2125
San Francisco, CA 94105
Telephone: 415-536-0288
Web site: http://www.iapsc.org
Area of expertise/focus: Security consulting
Membership: Open to those meeting qualifications

The purpose of the International Association of Professional Security Consultants (IAPSC) is to establish and maintain the highest possible standards in the security consulting profession. For that purpose, the association will provide opportunities for the professional enhancement of its members, and will promote greater awareness of the objective standards of its membership.

International Intelligence Network (INTELLENET)

P.O. Box 350
Gladwyne, PA 19035
Telephone: 610-520-9222
Web site: http://www.intelnetwork.org
Area of expertise/focus: Investigators and security consultants

Membership: Open to those meeting qualifications

Training: Seminars, conventions, and training experiences available through INTELLENET activities and other related associations

INTELLENET—is a worldwide network of investigators and security consultants. Our selective membership is restricted to individuals with extensive experience in law enforcement, investigations, intelligence, or private security. We offer an assortment of diversified services, and operational scopes are virtually unlimited throughout the U.S. and abroad.

International Association of Computer Investigative Specialist

PO Box 140

Donahue, IA 52846-0140

Web site: http://ists.dartmouth.edu/

Area of expertise/focus: Law enforcement professionals

Membership: Federal, state, local, and international law enforcement

Certification: IACIS certified forensic computer examiner

Social media: Facebook

International Association of Computer Investigative Specialist (IACIS) is an international volunteer nonprofit corporation composed of law enforcement professionals dedicated to education in the field of forensic computer science. IACIS members represent federal, state, local, and international law enforcement professionals. Regular IACIS members have been trained in the forensic science of seizing and processing computer systems.

International Association of Chief of Police

515 North Washington Street

Alexandria, VA 22314

Telephone: 703-836-6767; 800-THE IACP

Web site: http://www.theiacp.org/

Area of expertise/focus: Law enforcement professionals

Membership: Active or associate memberships open to police officers who qualify $120

Training: Center for Police Leadership and Training leadership programs; online training; grant funded low-cost training

Social media: Facebook; LinkedIn

The International Association of Chief of Police (IACP) is a dynamic organization that serves as the professional voice of law enforcement. Building on our past success, the IACP addresses cutting edge issues confronting law enforcement though advocacy, programs, and research, as well as training and other professional services. IACP is a comprehensive professional organization that supports the law enforcement leaders of today and develops the leaders of tomorrow.

International Association for Counterterrorism & Security Professionals

PO Box 100688
Arlington, VA 22210
Telephone: 212-362-3151
Web site: http://www.iacsp.com/main.php
Area of expertise/focus: Counterterrorism
Membership: $65
International Association for Counterterrorism & Security Professionals (IACSP) IACSP goals include creating a center of information and educational services for those concerned about the challenges now facing all free societies, and promoting professional ethics in the counterterrorism field.

International Association for Healthcare Security and Safety

PO Box 5038
Glendale Heights, IL 60139
Telephone: 630-871-9936
Web site: http://www.iahss.org/
Area of expertise/focus: Health care security and safety
Membership: Senior, partner, and associate memberships
Training: Conferences and seminars
The International Association for Healthcare Security and Safety, or IAHSS for short, is the only organization solely dedicated to professionals involved in managing and directing security and safety programs in health care institutions. IAHSS is comprised of security, law enforcement, and safety individuals dedicated to the protection of health care facilities worldwide.

International Association of Campus Law Enforcement Administrators

Web site: http://www.iaclea.org
Area of expertise/focus: Campus law enforcement
Membership: Professional $100; associate $60; affiliate $100; supporting $300; retired $30
Training: Annual and regional conferences
Social media: Facebook
The International Association of Campus Law Enforcement Administrators (IACLEA) advances public safety for educational institutions by providing educational resources, advocacy, and professional development services. IACLEA is a leading voice for the campus public safety community.

International Association of Financial Crimes Investigators

1020 Suncast Lane, Suite 102
El Dorado Hills, CA 95762
Telephone: 916-939-5000
Web site: http://www.iafci.org
Area of expertise/focus: Fraud investigation and prevention
Membership: Membership for those meeting qualifications. Regular $120; law enforcement $70
Training: Annual and regional conferences
The association, a nonprofit international organization, provides services and an environment within which information about financial fraud, fraud investigation, and fraud prevention methods can be collected, exchanged, and taught for the common good of the financial payment industry and our global society.

International Association of Law Enforcement Intelligence Analysts

PO Box 13857
Richmond, VA 23225
Web site: http://www.ialeia.org
Area of expertise/focus: Law enforcement professionals
Certification: Criminal intelligence certified analyst
Training: Conferences
Social media: Facebook; LinkedIn
The International Association of Law Enforcement Intelligence Analysts (IALEIA) is the largest professional organization in the world representing law enforcement analysts. It is based in the United States, and is a nonprofit 501(c) 3 corporation. IALEIA strives to capture the intelligence analysis experience of individuals and agencies and to convert and share that knowledge through law enforcement educational products.

International Association of Professional Security Consultants

575 Market St., Suite 2125
San Francisco, CA 94105
Telephone: 415-536-0288
Web site: http://www.iapsc.org/
Area of expertise/focus: Security consulting
Membership: Security consultants who meet qualifications
The purpose of the International Association of Professional Security Consultants (IAPSC) is to establish and maintain the highest possible standards in the security consulting profession. For that purpose, the association will provide opportunities for the professional enhancement of its members, and will promote greater awareness of the objective standards of its membership.

International Association of Special Investigation Units

PO Box 26
Manchester, MD 21102
8015 Corporate Drive, Suite A
Baltimore, MD 21236
Telephone: 443-507-6500
Web site: https://www.iasiu.org/
Area of expertise/focus: Insurance fraud
Membership: Members $200; nonmembers $400
Certifications: Certified insurance fraud investigator; certified insurance fraud analyst
Training: Online training center

Founded in 1984 by a handful of insurance industry fraud investigators, the International Association of Special Investigation Units (IASIU) is a nonprofit organization dedicated to promoting a coordinated effort within the industry to combat insurance fraud, providing education and training for insurance investigator, developing greater awareness of the insurance fraud problem, encouraging high professional standards of conduct among insurance investigators; and supporting legislation that acts as a deterrent to the crime of insurance fraud.

International Cargo Security Council

Telephone: 202-452-1200
Web site: http://www.ebroadcastcenter.com/icsc/
Area of expertise/focus: Cargo transportation; supply chain

The International Cargo Security Council is an association of professionals active in intermodal transportation and supply chain security. Its success hinges on each member's personal concern for the safe and secure movement of the nation's commerce.

International Foundation for Cultural Property Protection

Telephone: 800-257-6717
Web site: http://www.ifcpp.org
Area of expertise/focus: Protection of institutions
Membership: Individual, institutional, associate membership
Certification: Certified institutional protection manager
Training: Annual conference; certification class
Social media: Facebook; LinkedIn

The International Foundation for Cultural Property Protection provides an opportunity for professionals involved in the protection of cultural, educational, and public institutions to further professional development, access timely training, gain insight, and information about technology and industry advancements, network with peers, promote the sharing of resources, and enhance ethical practices.

International Foundation for Protection Officers

PO Box 771329
Naples, FL 34107
Telephone: 239-430-0534
Web site: http://www.ifpo.org
Area of expertise/focus: Security guard training
Membership: Associate, corporate, student, introductory memberships
Certifications: Certified protection officer (CPO), certified protection officer instructor (CPOI), certified security supervisor and management (CSSM)
Training: Classroom
Social media: Facebook

The International Foundation for Protection Officers (IFPO) is dedicated to providing meaningful and cost-effective security training for security guards and protection officers. The IFPO believes that education is a necessary and essential part of professional security training and the security officer's background. IFPO serves individuals, security companies, and organizations that have their own private security staff.

International Organization of Black Security Executives

Telephone: 925-222-0552
Web site: http://www.iobse.com/
Area of expertise/focus: Minority security professionals
Membership: Active $100; associate $50; student $25
Training: Annual conference
Social media: Facebook

The International Organization of Black Security Executives was founded in 1982 by Black Security Executives concerned about the relatively small number of minority professionals, and the role black security professionals could have in helping young people.

International Professional Security Association

Railway House
Railway Road Chorley
England P46 0HW
Telephone: 0845 873 8114; 1257 249945
Web site: http://ipsa.org.uk/
Area of expertise/focus: Security professionals
Membership: For individuals and companies working in security associated roles
Training: Courses for frontline staff, office staff, and trainers
Social media: Facebook

International Professional Security Association (IPSA), an established and recognized worldwide professional organization, provides, in accordance with growing demand, a specialized, unrivaled service to industry/commerce. There are no geographical boundaries in operation and the highest technical standards are stringently applied in all IPSA dealings.

International Security Management Association

Telephone: 563-381-4008
Web site: https://www.isma.com/
Area of expertise/focus: Security professionals
Membership: Stringent membership requirements
Training: International Security Management Association (ISMA) leadership program; conferences

ISMA is a premier international security association of senior security executives from major business organizations located worldwide. ISMA's mission is to provide and support an international forum of selected security executives whose combined expertise will be utilized in a synergistic manner in developing, organizing, assimilating, and sharing knowledge within security disciplines for the ultimate purpose of enhancing professional and business standards.

ISACA (formerly known as the Information Systems Audit and Control Association)

3701 Algonquin Road, Suite 1010
Rolling Meadows, Illinois 60008
Telephone: 847.253.1545
Web site: http://www.isaca.org/
Area of expertise/focus: Information technology; information systems professionals
Membership: Professional, student, academic memberships certifications:
Certifications: Certified information systems auditor (CISA); certified information security manager (CISM); certified in the governance of enterprise information technology (CGEIT); certified in risk and information systems control (CRISC)
Training: Conferences; online, onsite

ISACA sponsors international conferences, publishes the *Information Systems Control Journal*®, develops international information systems auditing and control standards, and administers the globally respected certified information systems auditor™ (CISA®) designation and the CISM® designation.

As a nonprofit, global membership association for IT and information systems professionals, ISACA is committed to providing its diverse constituency of more than 100,000 worldwide with the tools they need to achieve individual and organizational success.

Information Systems Security Association

220 SW Barbur Blvd, #119-333
Portland, OR 97219

Telephone: 866-349-5818 (toll free); 206-388-4584 (local/international)
Web site: http://www.issa.org
Area of expertise/focus: Information systems
Training: Executive forums; Webinars; events
Social media: Facebook

ISSA® is a not-for-profit, international organization of information security professionals and practitioners. It provides educational forums, publications, and peer interaction opportunities that enhance the knowledge, skill, and professional growth of its members.

(ISC)^2

1964 Gallows Road, Ste 210
Vienna, VA 22182
Telephone: 866-462-4777; 703-891-6781
Web site: http://www.isc2.org
Area of expertise/focus: Information systems
Certifications: Systems security certified practitioner (SSCP), certified authorization professional (CAP), certified secure software lifecycle professional (CSSLP), certified information system security professional (CISSP), certified cyber forensics professional (CCFP)
Training: Certification training
Social media: Twitter: @ISC^2; Facebook; LinkedIn

Headquartered in the United States and with offices in London, Hong Kong, and Tokyo, the International Information Systems Security Certification Consortium, Inc., (ISC)^2, is a global, not-for-profit leader in educating and certifying information security professionals.

Jewelers' Security Alliance

6 East 45th Street
New York, NY 10017, USA
Telephone: 800-537-0067
Web site: http://www.jewelerssecurity.org
Area of expertise/focus: Jewelry trade association
Social media: Facebook

The Jewelers' Security Alliance (JSA) is a non-profit trade association with 21,000 members that has been providing crime information and assistance to the jewelry industry and law enforcement since 1883. JSA fulfills its mission of informing and alerting jewelers about crime through frequent e-mail crime alerts and print publication, a Web site, seminars, and consulting activities. JSA also works closely with the FBI and local law enforcement agencies, sharing its data and analysis in order to further the war on jewelry crime.

Loss Prevention Foundation

700 Matthews Mint Hill Road, Suite C
Mathews, NC 28105
Telephone: 704-405-4404 or 866-433-5545
Web site: http://www.losspreventionfoundation.org/
Area of expertise/focus: Retail loss prevention
Membership: $25–$495
Certifications: LPQualified (LPQ) and LPCertified (LPC)
Training: Annual conference
Social media: Facebook

The Loss Prevention Foundation (LPF) is an international leader in educating and certifying retail loss prevention professionals. LPF's mission and passion is to advance the retail loss prevention and asset protection profession by providing relevant, convenient, and challenging educational resources.

Loss Prevention Research Council

Web site: http://www.lpresearch.org
Area of expertise/focus: Loss prevention
Social media: LinkedIn

The Loss Prevention Research Council (LPRC) was founded in 2001 by leading retailers in an effort to support the fact-based needs of the loss prevention industry. To date, the LPRC has conducted over 40 real-world loss prevention research projects for retailers and partners. The Council's research involves industry publications, research literature, members, innovative suppliers, academia, and in-house data. The LPRC explores, develops, and measures the loss reduction and financial impact of these initiatives using scientific methods.

Marine Embassy Guard Association

Web site: http://www.embassymarine.org
Area of expertise/focus: Military
Membership: Membership shall be open to marines who have served on active duty in the ranks of the United States Marine Corps
Social media: Facebook; LinkedIn

The Marine Embassy Guard Association (MEGA) is comprised of United States marines who have formerly served or are currently serving as marine guards since the inception of the program in 1948.

Maritime Security Council

P.O. Box 472627
Charlotte, NC 28247-2627
Telephone: 704-234-2600

Web site: http://www.maritimesecurity.org/
Area of expertise/focus: Maritime security
Membership: Membership open to those in maritime industry
Social media: Facebook; LinkedIn

The Maritime Security Council—established in 1988—is a nonprofit, member-driven organization representing ocean carriers, cruise lines, port facilities, and terminals, logistics providers, importers, exporters, and related maritime industries throughout the world.

National Association of Investigative Specialists

PO Box 82148
Austin, TX 78708
Telephone: 512-719-3595
Web site: http://www.pimall.com/nais/nais.j.html
Area of expertise/focus: Private investigative professionals
Membership: $85
Social media: Facebook

The National Association of Investigative Specialists is an American trade association of private investigative professionals that focuses in on marketing investigative services, developing new investigative techniques, providing training programs for those in practice or those wishing to enter the profession, developing positive media coverage of the investigative profession, acting as a center for case referrals and positive publicity referrals to members, and providing the overall membership with group buying power.

National Association of Professional Background Screeners

2501 Aerial Center Parkway, Suite 103
Morrisville, NC 27560
Telephone: 919-459-2082
Web site: http://www.napbs.com/
Area of expertise/focus: Background screening
Membership: Regular, associate, affiliate, international memberships
Training: Conferences and events
Social media: Facebook

The National Association of Professional Background Screeners exists to promote ethical business practices, compliance with the Fair Credit Reporting Act, equal employment opportunity, and state consumer protection laws relating to the background screening profession.

National Association of Retired Postal Inspectors

Post Office Box 3223
Peachtree City, GA 30269-7223
Web site: http://www.narpi.org

Area of expertise/focus: Postal employees

The National Association of Retired Postal Inspectors was founded in 1967 for the purpose of providing retired postal inspectors, their spouses, and other designated retired Postal Inspection Service employees and spouses a vehicle for social fellowship and recreational activities in their retirement years.

National Association of Security Companies

1651 Prince Street, Suite B
Alexandria, VA 22314
Telephone: 703-519-0912
Web site: http://www.nasco.org
Area of expertise/focus: Private security trade association
Training: Annual summit meeting
Social media: Facebook

The National Association of Security Companies (NASCO) is the nation's largest contract security trade association, representing private security companies that employ more than 250,000 of the nation's most highly trained security officers servicing every business sector. NASCO is leading the efforts to set meaningful standards for the private security industry and security officers by monitoring state and federal legislation and regulations affecting the quality and effectiveness of private security services.

National Association of Women Law Enforcement Executives

160 Lawrenceville-Pennington Road, Suite 16-115
Lawrenceville, NJ 08648
Telephone: 973-975-6146
Web site: http://www.nawlee.com/
Area of expertise/focus: Women law enforcement professionals
Membership: Executive and associate
Training: Annual national conference; mentoring program
Social media: Facebook; LinkedIn

The National Association of Women Law Enforcement Executives (NAWLEE) is the first organization established to address the unique needs of women holding senior management positions in law enforcement. NAWLEE is a nonprofit organization sponsored and administered directly by law enforcement practitioners. Its mission is to serve and further the interests of women executives and those who aspire to be executives in law enforcement.

National Association for Bank Security

Profit Protection, LLC
4800 SW 51st Street
Fort Lauderdale, FL 33314-3511
Telephone: 954-327-1223
Web site: www.banksecurity.com

Area of expertise/focus: Financial institution security and risk management

Training: Onsite

Profit protection, LLC, also very familiarly known as the National Association for Bank Security, is a financial institution security and risk management educational and consulting firm that has served the industry for more than 25 years with its products and services. Those services are offered in not only all areas of security governed by the mandates of the five financial institution regulators, but all facets of Bank Secrecy Act regulation requirements as well.

National Fire Protection Association

1 Batterymarch Park
Quincy, MA 02169
Telephone: 617-770-3000
Web site: http://www.nfpa.org
Area of expertise/focus: Fire prevention
Membership: $165/year
Training: Annual conference and expo; seminars; Webinars; on-site seminars; self-guided online courses
Social media: Facebook; LinkedIn

The mission of the international nonprofit National Fire Protection Association (NFPA), established in 1896, is to reduce the worldwide burden of fire and other hazards on the quality of life by providing and advocating consensus codes and standards, research, training, and education.

National Food Service Security Council

PO Box 1725
Olney, MD 20830
Telephone: 240-252-5542
Web site: http://www.nfssc.com/
Area of expertise/focus: Restaurant industry
Membership: Restaurant; franchisee/operator; vendor/service provider memberships
Training: Annual conference
Social media: LinkedIn

The National Food Service Security Council is a professional trade association of loss prevention, security, risk management, and safety professionals from the casual dining and quick serve restaurant industries.

National Organization of Black Law Enforcement Executives

4609-F Pinecrest Office Park Drive
Alexandria, VA 22312-1442
Telephone: (703) 658-1529
Web site: http://www.noblenational.org

Area of expertise/focus: Law enforcement professionals
Membership: Individual and business memberships
Training: Annual conference
Social media: Facebook; LinkedIn

National Organization of Black Law Enforcement Executives' (NOBLE's) mission is to ensure equity in the administration of justice, in the provision of public service to all communities, and to serve as the conscience of law enforcement by being committed to justice by action. The goal of NOBLE is to be recognized as a highly competent, public service organization that is at the forefront of providing solutions to law enforcement issues and concerns, as well as to the ever-changing needs of our communities.

National Sheriff's Association

1450 Duke Street
Alexandria, VA 22314
Telephone: 703-836-7827
Web site: http://www.sheriffs.org
Area of expertise/focus: Law enforcement professionals
Membership: Active $47–515; auxiliary $37–$62
Training: Law enforcement operations; court security; jail operations; domestic violence; National Sheriffs' Institute; Officer Leadership Program; Sheriff Training Partners
Social media: Facebook; LinkedIn

Chartered in 1940, the National Sheriffs' Association (NSA) is a professional association dedicated to serving the Office of Sheriff and its affiliates through police education, police training, and general law enforcement information resources. NSA represents thousands of sheriffs, deputies, and other law enforcement, public safety professionals, and concerned citizens nationwide.

Network Security Management Benchmarking Association

Telephone: 281-440-5044
Web site: http://www.nsmba.com/
Area of expertise/focus: Network security benchmarking
Membership: Open to individuals employed as permanent employees of companies

Network Security Management Benchmarking Association is dedicated to the analysis and improvement of business processes in network security. Through the exchange of data gathered in benchmarking surveys, members will be able to benefit from the experience of many companies.

Operations Security Professionals Society

PO Box 150515
Alexandria, VA 22315-0515
Telephone: 540-338-3048

Web site: http://www.opsecsociety.org
Area of expertise/focus: Operational security
Membership: Individual, corporate, government partnership
Certifications: Operations Security Professionals Society (OPSEC) certified professional (OCP); OPSEC associate professional (OAP)

OPSEC is the only association providing professional certifications and credentialing in the field of OPSEC. The Society's mission extends beyond members and attempts to help organizations understand and enable proper application of this mission-enhancing discipline.

Overseas Security Advisory Council

Bureau of Diplomatic Security
U.S. Department of State
Washington, DC 20522
Telephone: 571-345-2223
Web site: http://www.osac.gov
Area of expertise/focus: Government authority
Social media: Facebook; LinkedIn

The Overseas Security Advisory Council was created in 1985 under the Federal Advisory Committee Act to promote security cooperation between American private sector interests worldwide and the U.S. Department of State. The member organizations designate representatives to serve on the Overseas Security Advisory Council to provide direction and guidance to develop programs that most benefit the U.S. private sector overseas.

Pharmaceutical Security Institute

8100 Boone Blvd., Suite 220
Vienna, VA 22182
Telephone: 703-848-0160
Web site: http://www.psi-inc.org
Area of expertise/focus: Pharmaceuticals

The Pharmaceutical Security Institute is a not-for-profit, membership organization dedicated to protecting public health, sharing information on the counterfeiting of pharmaceuticals, and initiating enforcement actions through the appropriate authorities.

Risk and Security Management Forum

Web site: http://www.rsmf.co.uk/
Area of expertise/focus: Risk management
Training: Seminars

The Risk and Security Management Forum has about 60 plus members. It draws on their expertise to enhance risk management in government, law enforcement, the protective security services, corporate security, and commercially provided intelligence services.

Security Professionals Information Exchange

Bankers Hall
PO Box 22394 Calgary Alberta
T2P 4J1
Web site: http://www.spie.ca
Area of expertise/focus: Security professionals
Membership: Large or small organizations, consultants, educators, public sector, vendors
Training: Events
The Calgary Security Professionals Information Exchange Society is a Calgary, Alberta based organization created to improve access to information for local security professionals.

Society of Competitive Intelligence Professionals

PO Box 277
Falls Church, VA 22020
Telephone: 703-739-0696
Web site: http://www.scip.org/
Area of expertise/focus: Competitive intelligence
Membership: Individual $295; group $240; individual solutions provider $345; student $75; faculty/nonprofit $195
Certification: Society of Competitive Intelligence Professionals (SCIP) competitive intelligence professional (CIP)
SCIP's mission is to be the global organization of choice for professionals engaged in competitive intelligence and related disciplines; the premier advocate for the skilled use of intelligence to enhance business decision-making and organizational performance.

Society of Former Special Agents of the FBI, Inc.

3717 Fettler Park Drive
Dumfries, VA 22025
Telephone: 703-445-0026
Web site: http://www.socxfbi.org
Area of expertise/focus: FBI
Social media: Facebook
The mission of the Society is to promote the welfare of its members, preserve the friendships and loyalties achieved while special agents of the FBI and to support the FBI and law enforcement as positive forces in American society.

Society of Industrial Security Professionals

994 Old Eagle School Road, Suite 1019
Wayne, PA 19087

Telephone: 610-971-4856
Web site: http://www.classmgmt.com
Area of expertise/focus: Government and industrial security
Membership: $90
Certification: Industrial security professional (ISP) certification program
Training: Annual seminar
Social media: Facebook

The purpose of the Society of Industrial Security Professionals is to advance the practice of classification management in the disciplines of industrial security, information security, government designated unclassified information, and intellectual property, and to foster the highest qualities of security professionalism among its members.

Supply Chain Security and Loss Prevention Council of the American Trucking Association

950 North Glebe Road, Suite 210
Arlington, VA 22203-4181
Telephone: 703-838-1703
Web site: http://www.truckline.com/SCSL_Prevention_Council.aspx
Area of expertise/focus: Trucking industry
Training: Meetings, conferences, Webinars

The American Trucking Associations' (ATA) Supply Chain Security & Loss Prevention Council is the only national organization dedicated exclusively to addressing, establishing and advancing those policies and practices that achieve maximum security (supply chain personnel, cargo, truck, facility, information and the homeland); effective risk management and loss control, cargo theft reduction, successful claims management; and secure, non-violent work environments.

The Security Executive Council

Web site: https://www.securityexecutivecouncil.com/

The Security Executive Council is a leading problem-solving research and services organization focused on helping businesses build value while improving their ability to effectively manage and mitigate risk. Drawing on the collective knowledge of a large community of successful security practitioners, experts, and strategic alliance partners, the Council develops strategy, insight and identifies proven practices that cannot be found anywhere else. Our research, services, and tools are focused on protecting people, brand, information, physical assets, and the bottom line.

The Security Institute

4647 Stone Avenue
PO Box 5199

Sioux City, IA 51102-5199
Telephone: 712-274-6463
Web site: http://www.thesecurity-institute.org/
Area of expertise/focus: Emergency medical services
Training: Available online or by appointment
Social media: Facebook; LinkedIn
The Security Institute is designed to provide students and professional responders with an unprecedented standard of training in real-life, real-time conditions of crisis.

Transported Asset Protection Association

Web sites: http://www.tapaonline.org (Americas)
http://www.tapa-asia.org (Asia)
http://www.tapaeame.org (Europe, Africa, and Middle East)
http://www.tapabrasil.org.br (Brazil)
Area of expertise/focus: Technology
Membership: Full voting, associate, security service provider
Social media: Facebook; LinkedIn
As a worldwide coalition of manufacturers, shippers, carriers, insurers, service providers, law enforcement, and government agencies, Transported Asset Protection Association (TAPA) includes every type of company or organization facing the problem of cargo crime within the transportation supply chain. Our members work together to prevent these crimes through the sharing of information, development of supply chain security standards, and cooperation with government agencies.

Twin Cities Security Partnership

Minneapolis, MN
Web site: http://tc.securitypartnership.org
The Twin Cities Security Partnership is a public/private partnership dedicated to enhancing security, safety, and the quality of life in the greater twin cities area. It's a highly collaborative endeavor that brings together a broad spectrum of expertise and resources to build a stronger, safer community.

Women in Federal Law Enforcement

PMB-204 Suite 102
2200 Wilson Blvd.
Arlington, VA 22201
Telephone: 301-805-2180
Web site: http://wifle.wildapricot.org/
Area of expertise/focus: Law enforcement professionals
Social media: Facebook; LinkedIn
Women in Federal Law Enforcement (WIFLE) is a nonprofit organization open to women and men in law enforcement, supporters of WIFLE goals, government, and private industry individuals and organizations.

Women in International Security

c/o SIPRI North America
1111 19th Street, NW (12th Floor)
Washington, DC 20036
Telephone: 202-552-5401
Web site: http://wiisglobal.org/wordpress1/
Women in International Security (WIIS) remains the only global network actively advancing women's leadership, at all stages of their careers, in international peace and security.

Trade Publications
Campus Safety Magazine

Bobit Business Media
3520 Challenger Street
Torrance, CA 90503
Telephone: 310-533-2400
Fax: 310-533-2502
Web site: www.campussafetymagazine.com
E-mail: campussafetymagazine@bobit.com
Publication type: Online and bimonthly
Campus Safety magazine exclusively serves campus police chiefs, security directors, IT personnel, and executive administrators involved in the public safety and security of major hospitals, schools, and universities in the United States.

Canadian Security

240 Edward Street
Aurora, Ontario L4G 3S9
Telephone: 905-727-0077
Fax: 905-727-0017
Web site: www.candiansecuritymag.com
Canadian Security is a publication for professional security management in Canada, providing balanced editorial on issues relevant to end-users across all industry sectors.

Competitive Intelligence Magazine

1700 Diagonal Rd., Suite 600
Alexandria, VA 22314
Telephone: 703-739-0696
Fax: 703-739-2524
Web site: www.scip.org
E-mail: info@scip.org
Publication type: Bimonthly

Provides education and networking opportunities to business and competitive intelligence professionals (including marketing, market research, strategy, and information).

The Counter Terrorist Magazine

Kendall Tamiami Executive Airport
14300 S.W. 129th Street
Suite 204
Miami, FL 33186
Telephone: 866-573-3999
Fax: 786-573-2090
Web site: www.thecounterterroristmag.com/
E-mail: info@thecounterterroristmag.com
Publication type: Bimonthly

The *Counter Terrorist Magazine* is an information journal for homeland security professionals, providing first responders relevant technical information needed to combat terrorism at home and abroad.

CSO

CXO Media, Inc.
492 Old Connecticut Path
PO Box 9208
Framingham, MA 01701
Telephone: 508-872-0080
Fax: 508-879-7784
Web site: www.csoonline.com

CSO magazine is a resource for security executives who are active knowledge seekers on such topics as IT security, leadership, physical security, laws and compliance, business continuity, risk analysis, and privacy. *CSO* and CSOonline.com are published by CXO Media Inc., which is an IDG (International Data Group) company.

Disaster Recovery Journal

Disaster Recovery Journal
PO Box 510110
St. Louis, MO 63151
Telephone: 314-894-0276
Fax: 314-894-7474
Web site: www.drj.com
E-mail: drj@drj.com
Publication type: Quarterly

Disaster Recovery Journal is published quarterly by Systems Support Inc. and is free to all qualified personnel in the United States and Canada involved in managing, preparing, or supervising contingency planning.

The Journal of Economic Crime Management

The Journal of Economic Crime Management (JECM) Editor
Utica College
1600 Burrstone Road
Utica, NY 13502
Telephone: None Listed
E-mail: ggordon@utica.edu or drebovich@utica.edu
Web site: www.utica.edu/academic/institutes/ecii/jecm/index.cfm
Publication type: Online journal, published quarterly
Online forum for the discussion of theory, research, policy, and practice relating to economic crime and fraud management. The journal is structured to focus on five themes relevant to economic crime and fraud management: economic crime, including cybercrime; law and public policy; management; research and analytical methods; and technology, including fraud detection and prevention and security technologies.

Federal Bureau of Investigation—Law Enforcement Bulletin

J. Edgar Hoover Building
935 Pennsylvania Avenue, NW
Washington, D.C. 20535-0001
Telephone: 202-324-3000
Web site: www.fbi.gov/publications/
Publication type: Monthly
For over 60 years, the Bulletin has provided readers with practical information on a variety of topics. Feature articles are written by experts on a variety of law enforcement topics from forensics to personnel management, from law to communications, and much more.

The Forensic Examiner

ACFEI
2750 East Sunshine Street
Springfield, MO 65804
Telephone: 417-881-3818
Fax: 417-881-4702
Web site: www.acfei.com
E-mail: Editor@acfei.com
Publication type: Quarterly
The Forensic Examiner is the official peer-reviewed journal of the American College of Forensic Examiners Institute. The role of the journal is the continued advancement of forensic examination and consultation across the many professional fields of our membership.

Fraud Magazine

ACFE World Headquarters
The Gregor Building
716 West Avenue
Austin, TX 78701
Telephone: 800-245-3321
Fax: 512-478-9297
Web site: www.fraud-magazine.com
E-mail: fraudmagazine@acfe.com
Publication type: Bimonthly

Fraud Magazine is devoted to timely, insightful articles on white-collar crime
and fraud examination techniques.

Keesing Journal of Documents & Identity

Keesing Referency Systems
Hogehilweg 13, 1101 CA Amsteradam-Zuidoost
PO Box 1118, 1000 BC Amsterdam
The Netherlands
Telephone: 31205641117
Fax: 31205641115
Web site: www.keesingref.com
E-mail: ref@keesing.nl
Publication type: Bimonthly

Keesing Journal of Documents & Identity is a bimonthly magazine providing
professional information to all parties active in the document security industry.

Loss Prevention

Loss Prevention
7436 Leharne Dr
Charlotte, NC 28270
Telephone: 704-365-5226
Fax: 704-365-1026
Web site: www.LPportal.com
E-mail: comments@losspreventionmagazine.com
Publication type: Bimonthly

Loss Prevention is a magazine dedicated to the loss prevention (LP) industry con-
taining information from the leading solutions providers serving the industry, links
to career opportunities, and much more.

Professional Security Magazine

JTC Associates Ltd.
4, Elms Lane,

Shareshill,
Wolverhampton,
WV10 7JS
Telephone:+44 (0) 1922 415233
Fax:+44 (0) 1922 415208
E-mail: info@jtc.u-net.com
Web site: www.professionalsecurity.co.uk
Publication Type: Online and magazine

Professional Security Magazine offers an online service for the security professional to access news, views, and information on the move, at home or abroad.

Risk UK

ProActiv Publications
PO Box 332
Dartford
DA1 9FF
Telephone: 0208 295 8308
Web site: www.risk-uk.com
Publication type: Online and magazine

The magazine addresses all aspects of risk that are faced by today's business community, assisting those responsible for the security, safety, and risk management of the UK's largest companies.

Security Director's Report

3 Park Avenue, 30th Floor
New York, NY 10016
Telephone: 212-244-0360
Fax: 212-564-0465
Web site: www.ioma.com
E-mail: subserve@ioma.com
Publication type: Published monthly by the Institute of Management & Administration, Inc.

Security Director's Report is a monthly management tool designed to help security directors keep pace with the rapidly evolving world of corporate security. Each issue includes alerts to critical news, important new security products, and up-to-date advice.

Security Executive

National Association of Security Companies
1651 Prince Street, Suite B
Alexandria, VA 22314

Telephone: 703-519-0912
E-mail: jricci@nasco.org
Web site: www.securityexecutive.org
Publication type: Bimonthly
Security Executive is published bimonthly by the NASCO. It is designed to provide practical information on all aspects of security management.

Security Management

1625 Prince Street
Alexandria, VA 22314
Telephone: 703-519-6200
Fax: 703-519-6299
Web site: www.securitymanagement.com
Security Management provides a forum within which security professionals can learn about industry trends and solutions, including security strategies, management techniques, and new technologies.

Security Management Today

CMP Information Ltd
7th Floor, Ludgate House
245 Blackfriars Road
London SE1 9UY
Telephone: (44) 020 7921 8286
Web site: www.info4security.com
Publication type: Online and magazine
Security Management Today is specifically designed for security end-users seeking information on managing security including security management news, security product news releases, a dedicated Security Industry Authority (SIA) regulation section and an industry group section with up-to-date information on security industry news. Other key features include profiles of leading security management and case studies of the best practice in security system management.

SIU Today

IASIU Headquarters
8015 Corporate Drive
Suite A
Baltimore, MD 21236
Telephone: 410-931-3332
Fax: 410-931-2060
E-mail: info@iasiu.org
Web site: www.iasiu.org
Publication type: Quarterly

SIU Today is written and edited specifically for members of the International Association of Special Investigation Units. Each quarter, the magazine covers issues and trends relevant to deterring and uncovering insurance fraud. IASIU's quarterly magazine covers a wide variety of topics from legislative and law updates to regular features dealing with different fraud schemes, new resources, or individual company success stories.

Job Listing Sites for Security and Law Enforcement Professionals

Table 6.1 Job Listing Sites

Acronym	Organization Name	Web Site	Job Postings
ACFE	Association of Certified Fraud Examiners	www.cfenet.com	Open to public
AFIO	Association of Former Intelligence Officers	www.afio.com	Open to public
ASIS	ASIS International	www.asisonline.org	Membership only
CANASA	Canadian Security Association	www.canasa.org	Open to public
	CSO Magazine	www.csoonline.com	Open to public
ISSA	Information Systems Security Association	www.issa.org	Open to public
IACP	International Association of Chiefs of Police	www.theiacp.org	Open to public
IAFCI	International Association of Financial Crimes Investigators	www.iafci.org	Membership only
IALEIA	International Association of Law Enforcement Intelligence Analysts	www.ialeia.org	Open to public
IAPP	International Association of Privacy Professionals	www.privacyassociation.org	Open to public
ICSC	International Cargo Security Council	http://www.security-technologynews.com/suppliers/international-cargo-security-council-icsc.html icsc.html	Open to public
IECLEA	International Association of Campus Law Enforcement Administrators	www.iaclea.org	Open to public

Continued

Table 6.1 Job Listing Sites—cont'd

Acronym	Organization Name	Web Site	Job Postings
IFPO	International Foundation for Protection Officers	www.ifpo.org	Open to public
IPSA	International Professional Security Association	www.ipsa.org.uk	Open to public
ISMA	International Security Management Association	www.isma.com	Membership only
ISC^2	ISC^2	www.isc2.org	Open to public
	LinkedIn	www.linkedin.com	Open to public
	Monster	www.monster.com	Open to public
NFSSC	National Food Service Security Council	www.nfssconline.org	Open to public
NSA	National Sheriff's Association	www.sheriffs.org	Open to public
SEC	Security Executive Council	www.securityexecutivecouncil.com	Open to public
SJN	Security Jobs Network, Inc	www.securityjobs.net	Membership only
SCIP	Society of Competitive Intelligence Professionals	www.scip.org	Open to public
NCMS	Society of Industrial Security Professionals	www.classmgmt.com	Membership only
TAPA-Americas	Technical Asset Protection Association	www.tapaonline.org	Open to public
WIFLE	Women in Federal Law Enforcement	www.wifle.org	Open to public

Certifications

Table 6.2 Certifications

Initials	Certification Name	Issuing Organization
ABCP	Associate business continuity professional	DRI International
ARM	Associate in risk management	The Risk Management Society (RIMS)
BSCP	Building security certified professional	Building Security Certification Program
CAP	Certified authorization professional	ISC^2
CBCP	Certified business continuity professional	DRI International
CCFP	Certified cyber forensics professional	ISC^2

Table 6.2 Certifications—cont'd

Initials	Certification Name	Issuing Organization
CCI	Certified criminal investigator	American College of Forensic Examiners Institute
CCSP	Certified cargo security professional	North American Transportation Management Institute
CFCE	Certified forensic computer examiner	International Association of Computer Investigative Specialists
CFCP	Certified functional continuity professional	DRI International
CFE	Certified fraud examiner	Association of Certified Fraud Examiners
CFI	Certified forensic interviewer	International Association of Interviewers
CFI	Certified forensic investigator	Association of Certified Forensic Investigators of Canada
CGEIT	Certified in the governance of enterprise IT	International Systems Audit and Control Association
CHPA	Certified healthcare protection administrator	International Association for Healthcare Security & Safety
CHS	Certified in homeland security	American Board for Certification in Homeland Security
CICA	Criminal intelligence certified analyst	International Association of Law Enforcement Intelligence Analysts
CIFA	Certified insurance fraud analyst	International Association of Special Investigation Units
CIFI	Certified insurance fraud investigator	International Association of Special Investigation Units
CIPI	Certified institutional protection instructor	International Foundation for Cultural Property Protection
CIPM	Certified institutional protection manager	International Foundation for Cultural Property Protection
CIPS	Certified institutional protection specialist	International Foundation for Cultural Property Protection
CIPT	Certified institutional protection technician	International Foundation for Cultural Property Protection
CISA	Certified information systems auditor	Information Systems Audit and Control Association
CISM	Certified information security manager	Information Systems Audit and Control Association
CISSP	Certified information system security professional	(ISC)^2
CLSD	Certified lodging security director	American Hotel & Lodging Educational Institute
CLSO	Certified lodging security officer	American Hotel & Lodging Educational Institute

Continued

Table 6.2 Certifications—cont'd

Initials	Certification Name	Issuing Organization
CLSS	Certified lodging security supervisor	American Hotel & Lodging Educational Institute
CPA	Certified public Accountant	American Institute of Certified Public Accountants
CPO	Certified protection officer	International Foundation for Protection Officers
CPOI	Certified protection officer instructor	International Foundation for Protection Officers
CPP	Certified protection professional	ASIS International
CRISC	Certified in risk and information systems control	International Systems Audit and Control Association
CSSLP	Certified secure software lifecycle professional	ISC^2
CSSM	Certified in security supervision and management	International Foundation for Protection officers
FSO	Facilities security officer	U.S. Department of Defense/Defense Security Service
ISP	Industrial security professional	The Society of Industrial Security Professionals
LPC	LPCertified	Loss Prevention Foundation
LPQ	LPQualified	Loss Prevention Foundation
MBCP	Master business continuity professional	DRI International
OAP	OPSEC associate professional	OPSEC Professionals Society
OPC	OPSEC certified professional	OPSEC Professionals Society
PCI	Professional certified investigator	ASIS International
PSP	Physical security professional	ASIS International
SCIP CIP	SCIP competitive intelligence professional	Society of Competitive Intelligence Professionals
SSCP	Systems security certified practitioner	ISC^2

ABCP—Associate Business Continuity Professional

DRI International

www.drii.org

The ABCP level is for individuals with less than two years of industry experience, but who have minimum knowledge in business continuity management, and have successfully passed the qualifying exam.

ARM—Associate in Risk Management

The Risk Management Society

www.aicpcu.org

The new ARM program teaches the in-depth knowledge needed to assess and respond to the numerous hazard risks your company faces.

BSCP—Building Security Certified Professional

Building Security Council

www.buildingsecuritycouncil.org

BSCP certification designates licensed design professionals (architects, landscape architects, and engineers), PSP, and CPP who demonstrate, by means of a detailed application and written examination, knowledge and understanding of the multidisciplinary security considerations that are relevant to the integrated planning, design, construction, operation, and evaluation of buildings, as identified by the BSC PLUS Rating System.

CAP—Certified Authorization Professional

ISC^2

www.isc2.org

The CAP certification is an objective measure of the knowledge, skills, and abilities required for personnel involved in the process of authorizing and maintaining information systems. Specifically, this credential applies to those responsible for formalizing processes used to assess risk and establish security requirements and documentation.

CBCP—Certified Business Continuity Professional

DRI International

www.drii.org

The CBCP level of certification is for individuals who have demonstrated knowledge and working experience in the business continuity/disaster recovery industry.

CCFP—Certified Cyber Forensics Professional

ISC^2

www.isc2.org

The CCFP credential indicates expertise in forensics techniques and procedures, standards of practice, and legal and ethical principles to assure accurate, complete, and reliable digital evidence admissible to a court of law. It also indicates the ability to apply forensics to other information security disciplines, such as e-discovery, malware analysis, or incident response.

CCI—Certified Criminal Investigator

American College of Forensic Examiners Institute

www.acfei.com

Investigating criminal behavior involves many different facets. Investigators must identify the crime scene, look for evidence, conduct interviews, properly identify and handle evidence, and testify in court.

CCSP—Certified Cargo Security Professional

American Trucking Association
North American Transportation Management Institute
The CCSP credential recognizes proficiency in 11 key trucking security domains and provides security professionals with the expert knowledge and industry tools to assess and manage risk, and protect personnel, assets and cargo.

CFCE—Certified Forensic Computer Examiner

International Association of Computer Investigative Specialist
www.cops.org
The CFCE Training and Certification programs are based on a series of competencies. In late 2009, the training, standards, and certification committees met to update the CFCE certification competencies in an effort to align the objectives with current standards and practices in computer/digital forensics.

CFCP—Certified Functional Continuity Professional

DRI International
www.drii.org
The Certified Functional Continuity Professional is for those in our industry with a specific skill or focus. These individuals have demonstrated knowledge and skill in business continuity within a very narrow scope. An example of this would be an expert in IT recovery, application testing, or BIAs.

CFE—Certified Fraud Examiner

Association of Certified Fraud Examiners
www.cfenet.com
To earn the CFE credential, an individual must pass a test that focuses on the four major disciplines that comprise the fraud examination body of knowledge: fraud prevention and deterrence; fraudulent financial transactions; fraud investigation; and legal elements of fraud.

CFI—Certified Forensic Interviewer

International Association of Interviewers
www.certifiedinterviewer.com
The certified forensic interviewer (CFI) designation and examination came about through the work of professionals from both the public and private sector who foresaw the need to take the next step in the defense and professionalization of interviewers.

CFI—Certified Forensic Investigator

Association of Certified Forensic Investigators of Canada
www.acfi.ca/

Certified forensic investigators (CFIs) are professional fraud investigators who have by experience, education, and examination satisfied the requirements of the Association of Certified Forensic Investigators and have been admitted as regular members of the Association.

CGEIT—Certified in the Governance of Enterprise IT

International Systems Audit and Control Association
www.isaca.org
CGEIT recognizes a range of professionals for their knowledge and application of enterprise IT governance principles and practices. CGEIT provides you the credibility to discuss critical issues around governance and strategic alignment based on your recognized skills, knowledge, and business experience.

CHPA—Certified Healthcare Protection Administrator

International Association for Healthcare Security & Safety
www.iahss.org
The CHPA exam is administered by the Commission to those individuals successfully qualifying for the exam. Qualified candidates who apply and are accepted into the credentialing program will be at the graduate level.

CHS—Certified in Homeland Security

American Board for Certification in Homeland Security
www.abchs.com
The American Board for Certification in Homeland Security, CHS® (ABCHS), a professional membership association, has earned a reputation as a premier certification and continuing education source for professionals in homeland security. However, ABCHS membership is not required for certificants and candidates.

CIPI—Certified Institutional Protection Instructor

International Foundation for Cultural Property Protection
www.ifcpp.org
Designates qualified alarm, computer, communications, and other technology experts working in a cultural property protection or related environment, with primary responsibilities in technology-based duties and disciplines.

CIPM—Certified Institutional Protection Manager

International Foundation for Cultural Property Protection
www.ifcpp.org
Designates those managers, directors, administrators, or others responsible for the protection of a cultural facility or public institution. Candidates in this category

include contract or proprietary security managers, security directors, law enforcement officers, facility managers, or those ultimately responsible for protection of the facility.

CIPS—Certified Institutional Protection Specialist

International Foundation for Cultural Property Protection
www.ifcpp.org
Designates those line officers and midlevel supervisors working in, or directly responsible, for the protection of a cultural facility or public institution. This category includes proprietary or contract security officers, or other staff with additional duties in facility protection.

CIPT—Certified Institutional Protection Technician

International Foundation for Cultural Property Protection
www.ifcpp.org
Designates qualified alarm, computer, communications, and other technology experts working in a cultural property protection or related environment, with primary responsibilities in technology-based duties and disciplines.

CISA—Certified Information Systems Auditor

Information Systems Audit and Control Association
www.isaca.org
The CISA certification is world-renowned as the standard of achievement for those who audit, control, monitor, and assess an organization's information technology and business systems.

CISM—Certified Information Security Manager

Information Systems Audit and Control Association
www.isaca.org
The management-focused CISMis the globally accepted standard for individuals who design, build, and manage enterprise information security programs. CISM is a leading credential for information security managers.

CISSP—Certified Information System Security Professional

ISC^2
www.isc2.org
CISSP® certification is a globally recognized standard of achievement that confirms an individual's knowledge in the field of information security. CISSPs are information assurance professionals who define the architecture, design, management, and/or controls that assure the security of business environments.

CLSD—Certified Lodging Security Director

American Hotel & Lodging Educational Institute
www.ei-ahla.org
The CLSD designation provides recognition for essential property management expertise, sound judgment, and practical skills. Recognized worldwide, the CLSD designation is the lodging industry's highest acknowledgment of professionalism for security directors in the hospitality industry.

CLSO—Certified Lodging Security Officer

American Hotel & Lodging Educational Institute
www.ei-ahla.org
The CLSO is a competency-based certification program that recognizes lodging security officers for their knowledge and job performance. Through an assessment and testing process, a lodging security officer can earn a designation, which acknowledges competence in the duties they perform.

CLSS—Certified Lodging Security Supervisor

American Hotel & Lodging Educational Institute
www.ei-ahla.org
The CLSS® designation provides recognition for effective human resources and emergency management expertise as well as sound judgment and practical skills. Recognized worldwide, the CLSS® designation is the lodging industry's highest acknowledgment security supervisors in the hospitality industry.

CPA—Certified Public Accountant

American Institute of Certified Public Accountants
www.aicpa.org
One of the world's leading licensing examinations, the CPA examination serves to protect the public interest by helping to ensure that only qualified individuals become licensed as CPAs.

CPO—Certified Protection Officer

International Foundation for Protection Officers
www.ifpo.org
The CPO program is designed for protection professionals who are intent on improving their individual security skills.

CPOI—Certified Protection Officer Instructor

International Foundation for Protection Officers
www.ifpo.org
CPOIs are individuals who teach the CPO program or a portion thereof.

CPP—Certified Protection Professional

ASIS International

www.asisonline.org

The CPP® credential provides demonstrable proof of knowledge and management skills in eight key domains of security. Those who earn the CPP are ASIS board-certified in security management.

CRISC—Certified in Risk and Information Systems Control

International Systems Audit and Control Association

www.isaca.org

CRISC® (pronounced see-risk) is the only certification that positions IT professionals for future career growth by linking IT risk management to enterprise risk management, and positioning them to become strategic partners to the business.

CSSM—Certified Security Supervisor and Management

International Foundation for Protection Officers

www.ifpo.org

Completion of the security supervision and management program is a mandatory element of enrollment into the CSSM Program. Once the candidate has successfully completed the security supervision and management program, he or she may choose to apply to the IFPO to be accepted into the official CSSM certification program.

CSSLP—Certified Secure Software Lifecycle Professional

ISC^2

www.isc2.org

With the CSSLP® certification from ISC^2, your application security competency within the software development lifecycle will be validated. You will not only be seen as an industry leader in application security, but as a leader within your organization as well.

FSO—Facilities Security Officer

The FSO program management for FSOs at possessing facilities (facilities with approval to store classified material) curriculum complies with the training requirements stated in paragraph 3-102 of the *National Industrial Security Program Operating Manual* (NISPOM) (DoD 5220.22-M).

ISP—Industrial Security Professional

The Society of Industrial Security Professionals

www.classmgmt.com

The intent of the ISP designation is to award professional certification and recognition to qualified candidates who demonstrate the knowledge, skills, and abilities their profession demands. The basis for the examination is primarily the NISPOM, the supplements, and other information security concomitant rules and regulations to include operations security, proprietary information, and related topics.

LPC—LPCertified

Loss Prevention Foundation
www.losspreventionfoundation.org
The LPC is an advanced certification for experienced loss prevention/asset protection professionals that integrates the business of loss prevention into retail profit center practices and logistics.

LPQ—LPQualified

Loss Prevention Foundation
www.losspreventionfoundation.org
The LPQ is a benchmark certification that canvases loss prevention practices, core competencies, foundational tools, business processes, and best practices for today's LP professional. In conjunction, the LPF provides LPQ educational material in a college accredited, web accessible course.

MBCP—Master Business Continuity Professional

DRI International
www.drii.org
The MBCP is DRI International's highest level of certification and is reserved for individuals with significant demonstrated knowledge and skill in the business continuity/disaster recovery industry. The certification is tailored to individuals with at least five years of industry experience and demands a high level of industry commitment, as well as additional and continual enhancement of your knowledge and skill level.

OAP—OPSEC Association Professional

OPSEC Professionals Society
www.opsecsociety.org
The OAP category was created to facilitate the development of OPSEC Professionals Society (OPS) members as they progress toward the full certification status of OCP.

OPC—OPSEC Certified Professional

OPSEC Professionals Society
www.opsecsociety.org

The OPS established the OCP certification to support professional development and improvement through the exchange of ideas and information on the methods, practices, and procedures related to OPSEC programs and associated activities.

PCI—Professional Certified Investigator

ASIS International

www.asisonline.org

The PCI® credential provides demonstrable proof of an individual's knowledge and experience in case management, evidence collection, and preparation of reports and testimony to substantiate findings. Those who earn the PCI are ASIS board-certified in investigations.

PSP—Physical Security Professional

ASIS International

www.asisonline.org

The PSP® credential provides demonstrated knowledge and experience in threat assessment and risk analysis; integrated physical security systems; and the appropriate identification, implementation, and ongoing evaluation of security measures. Those who earn the PSP are ASIS board certified in physical security.

The PSP designation is awarded to individuals whose primary responsibilities are to conduct threat surveys; design integrated security systems that include equipment, procedures, and people; or install, operate, and maintain those systems.

SSCP—Systems Security Certified Practitioner

ISC^2

www.isc2.org

The SSCP is open to all candidates with as little as one year experience, making it an ideal starting point for a new career in information security or to add that layer of security you need in your current IT career.

About Elsevier's Security Executive Council Risk Management Portfolio

Elsevier's Security Executive Council Risk Management Portfolio is the voice of the security leader. It equips executives, practitioners, and educators with research-based, proven information and practical solutions for successful security and risk management programs. This portfolio covers topics in the areas of risk mitigation and assessment, ideation and implementation, and professional development. It brings trusted operational research, risk management advice, tactics, and tools to business professionals. Previously available only to the Security Executive Council community, this content—covering corporate security, enterprise crisis management, global information technology (IT) security, and more—provides real-world solutions and "how-to" applications. This portfolio enables business and security executives, security practitioners, and educators to implement new physical and digital risk management strategies and build successful security and risk management programs.

Elsevier's Security Executive Council Risk Management Portfolio is a key part of the **Elsevier Risk Management & Security Collection**. The collection provides a complete portfolio of titles for the business executive, practitioner, and educator by bringing together the best imprints in risk management, security leadership, digital forensics, IT security, physical security, homeland security, and emergency management: Syngress, which provides cutting-edge computer and information security material; Butterworth-Heinemann, the premier security, risk management, homeland security, and disaster-preparedness publisher; and Anderson Publishing, a leader in criminal justice publishing for more than 40 years. These imprints, along with the addition of Security Executive Council content, bring the work of highly regarded authors into one prestigious, complete collection.

The Security Executive Council (www.securityexecutivecouncil.com) is a leading problem-solving research and services organization focused on helping businesses build value while improving their ability to effectively manage and mitigate risk. Drawing on the collective knowledge of a large community of successful security practitioners, experts, and strategic alliance partners, the Council develops strategy and insight and identifies proven practices that cannot be found anywhere else. Their research, services, and tools are focused on protecting people, brand, information, physical assets, and the bottom line.

Elsevier (www.elsevier.com) is an international multimedia publishing company that provides world-class information and innovative solutions tools. It is part of Reed Elsevier, a world-leading provider of professional information solutions in the science, medical, risk, legal, and business sectors.

Index

Note: Page numbers with "*b*" denote boxes; "*f*" figures; "*t*" tables.

205

Printed and bound by CPI Group (UK) Ltd, Croydon, CR0 4YY

08/05/2025

01864909-0002